This book is brought to you with special thanks to  reat inspiration in my life and in the creation of this bo

Thank you to my friends and family, who have alwa , and to Chris Hanchey, who always creates great artwork.

Also, special thanks to the following entrepreneurs, start-ups, and businesses who were a great help while researching the book. It was a pleasure talking to you all and I include you here as an inspiration to others!

Fraser Doherty – Super Jam

Fraser built a successful jam business starting at the tender age of 14 and has since sold millions of jars. He says:

'After learning how to make jam from my Grandmother at 14 years old, I started selling homemade jam to the neighbours. Since then, I developed a way of making jam 100% from fruit and have since sold many millions of jars of Super Jam through thousands of stores around the world. My story shows that it is possible to start something on a tiny scale and with a bit of love, imagination and hard work, it can grow into something amazing – something that changes your life. My advice to anyone trying to start out in business would be to not be afraid of taking the first steps of trying in the first place, start small and find a mentor who can share what they have learned.'

http://shop.superjam.co.uk/

Zandra Johnson – Fairy Tale Children's Furniture

Zandra built a successful children's furniture business starting at the age of 67. She says:

'One of the characteristics Entrepreneurs (or Olderpreneurs) need is tenacity – lots of it. Every time I am working on a project, finding a solution to a problem or encountering yet another steep learning curve I keep telling myself, "You are not finished when you are defeated. You are only defeated when you quit.'

http://www.fairytalechildrensfurniture.co.uk

Ted Nash – Tapdaq.com

Ted is a 22 year-old English entrepreneur who sold £1m of apps via App Store downloads. He infamously created the million-selling apps Fit Or Fugly and Rack Share. He says:

'If you, as a young entrepreneur, believe you have the vision to make something remarkable, you need to develop a relentless passion for your business because when you fail you'll have the determination to get back up and try again. You have to fail before you succeed. Three words: vision, passion, determination.'

http://www.tapdaq.com/

Jessica Rose – London Jewellery School

Jessica built a successful jewellery tuition school five years ago at the age of 21, and now has premises in the famous Hatton Garden and runs a £500,000 turnover business. She says:

'I think the most important thing when starting a business is to choose something you are passionate about. So many people go in for the wrong reasons like trying to make a quick buck or for an easier/simpler life. Generally, these are the ones that don't get very far. It takes years for most businesses to take off and reach a decent level of profit and you will need to work hard every day to achieve your vision, so you want to be doing something that is meaningful to you and that you won't get bored of. Start with a clear and dedicated vision and the rest will follow. The rewards, once they come, will be more than worth it, and the freedom and excitement you get from running your own business is like nothing else. I have worked tirelessly for over four years to build the London Jewellery School to the successful business it is today. There have been many ups and downs and I have had my fair share of 70-hour weeks, but it is my true passion and I wouldn't change it for the world.'

http://www.londonjewelleryschool.co.uk

Also, additional thanks to these businesses and start-ups, some of which give their own words of wisdom:

(Please feel free to use these contacts for your own business).

Fashion, Art, Design

Isabelle Plasschaert http://bebelle.photoshelter.com London-based freelance photographer.

SpottinStyle.com http://www.spottinstyle.com A snapshot of the world's fashion.

Gil Kahana http://www.chattyfeet.com Let your Chatty Feet character socks out to play!

Terry Li http://www.terryliphotography.co.uk London wedding photographer.

Aarefa Tayabji http://www.behance.net/atjgraphics Graphic designer & creative artworker.

Jessica Lascar http://jexyla.com

Gary Lancet http://www.thinkinggifts.com Manufacturer of book accessories and stationery.

Web Design, Tech, SEO

Abid Kiani http://www.mtiwebdesign.co.uk Let us build your business.

Lanre Olaniba http://www.plugandplaydesign.co.uk/clapham
Read this book, get inspired, go digital, succeed.

Rob Cubbon http://robcubbon.com I'm a web designer and happy to help anyone :)

Mohammed Elalj http://www.refurb.me/ Get notifications on Apple refurbished products.

Alex Shaw http://www.controla.co.uk Web design, internet marketing training.

David Asfaha http://twitter.com/dasfaha Online digital marketing education.

Clarissa Sajbl http://www.linkdex.com Linkdex is an award-winning SaaS marketing platform.

Chandry Roychowdhury http://www.itsweb.co.uk Itsweb is a UK-based full service web designing company.

Edward Turay http://www.facebook.com/taaimestudios Success is just the beginning.

Gareth Hewitt http://whiteskystudio.com A new way to easily build cloud applications.

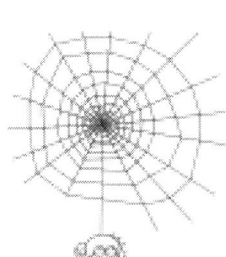

Video and Music

David Guerra-Terol http://videolean.com Build a business, not just a great product/service.

Iain Clark http://www.redpowerstation.co.uk Video speech training, production, sales pipelines.

Tom Woodall http://niceonefilm.com

Health, Food, Lifestyle

Yuda Galis http://www.privatepersonalchefs.co.uk We are a London personal chef service.

Sonal Shah http://www.synergynutrition.co.uk I live by the motto: Your HEALTH is your WEALTH.

Business, Professional Services

The Bakery http://www.thebakerylondon.com We match-make tech to brands business problems.

Valerie Chan http://www.vfaccountants.co.uk VF Accountants helping start-ups be tax efficient.

Bobby Keer http://www.leagoldmiller.co.uk Financial advisors and insurance brokers.

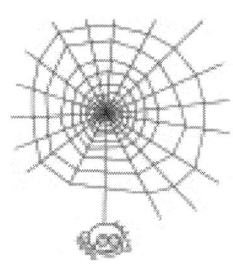

Joseph Warmann http://www.BizWizardry.com Get more sales with a lot less stress.

Razina Munim http://www.useyourcommunity.com Search for the free local services in your area.

Kiran Ramakrishna http://www.edit-place.co.uk/ Quality content for web companies in 17 languages.

Gordon Kelly http://gordonkelly.com Super heroes are apt for a super book!

Bespoke KubraTez http://bespokekubratez.tumblr.com/ I create bespoke interior design solutions.

Kate Barrett http://www.shinealightmedia.com Supercharging your email marketing!

6

Louis Sibbert   http://www.LondonMarketingLab.com Responsive Marketing with SMS text Messages

Lisa Newton http://www.booglesltd.com
Bookkeeping services.

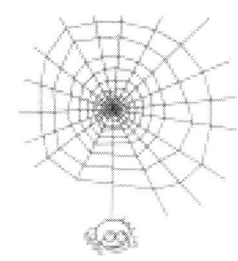

Products

Mike Hodgkinson http://www.fxbikes.com Mountain Moto... World's lightest motorcycles!

Ransford Davies-King http://www.standupproducts.co.uk
A very multi-functional Bluetooth iPhone stand.

Educational, Kids

Sue Atkins http://www.TheSueAtkins.com Put in 110% and focus on one thing.

Amanda Gummer http://www.goodtoyguide.com THE play advice site: toy reviews, expert advice.

Deepak Shukla http://www.meetmytutor.com/ If you need a tutor, go to our site Meet My Tutor.

Social

Karan Khemani http://www.bugscore.com/ Bugscore is an online scoring platform.

Paul Sipasseuth http://deparz.com Help people change their lives.

This book is designed to provide information and motivation to our readers. It is sold with the understanding that the publisher is not engaged to render any type of psychological, legal, or any other kind of professional advice. The content of the book is the sole expression and opinion of its author, and not necessarily that of the publisher. No warranties or guarantees are expressed or implied by the publisher's choice to include any of the content in this volume. Neither the publisher nor the individual author shall be liable for any physical, psychological, emotional, financial, or commercial damages, including, but not limited to, special, incidental, consequential, or other damages. Our views and rights are the same: you are responsible for your own choices, actions, and results.

The story and its characters and entities are fictional. Any likeness to actual persons, either living or dead, is strictly coincidental.

All trade marks are the property of their respective owners.
ZERO TO SUPERHERO® is a registered trade mark.

BUSINESS ZERO TO SUPERHERO ®.

LIMITED EDITION VERSION

Business Zero To Superhero ®
Copyright © 2019 by G. Jules

All rights reserved. No part of this publication may be reproduced, stored in a retrieval system, or transmitted by any means – electronic, mechanical, photographic (photocopying), recording, or otherwise – without prior permission in writing from the author. This book may not be lent, resold, hired out, or otherwise disposed of by way of trade in any form of binding or cover other than that in which it is published without the prior written consent of the publisher.

Written and produced in the United Kingdom
ISBN-13: 978-1490371610

ISBN-10: 1490371613

Get more information at:

www.business-zerotosuperhero.co.uk

www.zerotosuperhero.co.uk

www.facebook.com/businesszerotosuperhero

www.twitter.com/businesuperhero

www.grahamjules.co.uk

Contents

Thanks	1
Contents	14
About This Book	20
INTRODUCTION	25
INTRODUCTION (Comic Book Page 1)	25
Electric Dreams	27
Floppy Business	28
All Work and No Play	29
Surprise, Surprise	30
Hot Property 31	
Disaster, Darling	34
DISASTER DARLING (Comic Book Page 2)	33
BUSINESS ZERO (Comic Book Page 3)	35
Business Zero	35
STARTING OUT	37
Problem Solving	37
What You Really, Really Want?	41
Money, Money, Money	41
Free At Last	42
SLEEPING BEAUTY (Comic Book Page 4)	44
Sleeping Beauty	45
Problem Solving	46
Two's Company	49
Problem Solving	50
START UP COSTS	57

Money's Too Tight To Mention	57
Dirty Cash	58

COMPUTER SAYS NO (Comic Book Page 5)   60

Problem Solving   61
Computer Says No	67
Credit Where Credit Is Due	68
Virtual Insanity	70
Laughing On Judgement Day	71

Problem Solving   72
Spend, Spend , Spend	81
Buy, Beg, Or Steal	82

Problem Solving   83

WHAT TO SPEND ON?   86
We Can Work It Out	86

Problem Solving   88

HUMAN EQUATION (Comic Book Page 6)   95
DOING THE MATHS	95
Human Equation	96

Problem Solving   98

ORGANISING YOURSELF   102
Organised Confusion	102

YOUR DATABASE   104
Inspiration Information	104

TO CATCH A VIRUS (Comic Book Page 7)   106

MARKETING   106

To Catch A Virus	107
Email From Heaven	109
Problem Solving	111
YOUR TIME	115
Wiser For The time	115
High Priority	116
Relax, Don't Do It	118
POSITIVE THINKING	121
NEGATIVE ENERGY (Comic Book Page 8)	121
Good Vibrations	122
WEIRD STUFF	125
Spirit In The Sky	125
Wonders Of The Universe	126
HEALTH: PHYSICAL, AND MENTAL	128
In Sickness And In Health	128
Problem Solving: My Story	128
Food For Thought	133
The Drugs Don't Work	133
Mind Body And Soul	135
Stop The Negativity	136
REPUTATION (Comic Book Page 9)	138
REPUTATION	138
Public Image	139
Fix Up Look Sharp	141
Problem Solving	143
SEARCH ENGINES	151
SEARCH FOR THE HERO (Comic Book Page 10)	151
Search For The Hero	152

Press To Play	157
AUTOMATION	162
AUTOMATION (Comic Book Page 11)	162
Automation Baby	163
Licence To Thrill	165
INCREASE PROFIT OVERNIGHT	166
Profit Prophet	166
GOOGLE	168
Like An Ever Flowing Stream	168
Back On The Map	168
Word Up	169
KEEPING RECORDS	170
Paper, Scissors, Stone	170
RISK	174
RISKY BUSINESS (Comic Book Page 12)	174
Risky Business	175
SAVING/INVESTING	177
Saving Grace	177
HOW TO FIND INVESTORS	182
CITY OF ANGELS (Comic Book Page 13)	182
City Of Angels	183
In Search Of Angels	185
Tip: Free Investor List	186
Take My Tip	189
First Meeting	192
Hit The Deck	192
For You	195

MY STORY	182
Who Wants To Meet A Millionaire?	198
Lessons To Be Learned	204
The Answer	205
Big Plans	206
Foundations	210
THE FUNDING PANEL	211
21 Questions	211
Panel Tips	215
THE £250,000 PRESENTATION	216
Never Gonna Give You Up	216
Very Important People	217
Million Dollar Plan	220
The Three Angels	222
The Final Countdown	224
THE END (Comic Book Page 14)	230
THE END	231
ABOUT THE AUTHOR	233
Contact Information:	234
Notes:	236
Index	237
Bibliography	240

ABOUT THIS BOOK

What do I know? Well, I have dabbled in entrepreneurship for over twenty years. I am a Business Law LLB Graduate and have experienced my fair share of business challenges, for example, the making of this book! I will explain. As you are aware, this book is called Business Zero To Superhero®. Well, after writing the first draft in 2013, I decided to trade mark the title, a seemingly simple administrative process via the Intellectual Property Office, which I will cover later. However, after registering my shiny new book title, I received a letter from Marvel and DC Entertainments Inc (Creators of Superman, Batman et al.) solicitors, threatening opposition of the title. A near three-year legal battle ensued with one of the largest media and entertainment companies in the world! (Oops). All this, over the word, SUPERHEROES, which was the trade mark owned by Marvel and DC. So much for a 'simple' administrative process.

Metro Newspaper London 25 May 2016

Obviously, this was a huge shock, and it was very tempting just to cave in and change the title. However, I 'donned my cape', dug in my heels and fought to the end, and was delighted (and relieved) when Marvel and DC dropped the case, and my trade mark proceeded to full registration in May 2016 (phew).

So you see, this was a huge threat to this book's business model, the process took a huge amount of time and effort, but the resulting media exposure was great, and I appeared on Sky News, the BBC, and national as well as local news. By solving the problem, the rewards came. Not only did I have the registered trade mark, but I had also raised the profile of myself and the book. I had gone from Business Zero To Superhero ®!

Why should you read this book? Well, there are many business books that purport to enable you to become a millionaire or get rich quick. If you are looking for one of those, I suggest you put this book down NOW!

OK, so you're still reading, great! What many of these books lack is any insight at all as to how to create a business from scratch, from rock bottom and literally zero. More worryingly, many do not cover how to deal with the 'real world' problems you are likely to face as an entrepreneur, and instead concentrate on the sweet cocktail of multi-million pound deals, million pound investments, and fat bank accounts- all achievable within six months. If only…

This book deals with reality. THINGS <u>WILL</u> GO WRONG. I'm not saying this to scare you, honestly, but it is my opinion that 'real world' business is not about making money (gasp), but is really about solving problems (cry). No, I'm not saying you should not make any money, but I am suggesting that the difference in mindset can make the difference between success and failure. In a nutshell, people are willing to pay you to solve their problems, or if you can solve hard problems you will inevitably get paid. Once you make that shift in mindset, you will not get phased by business 'problems', but will view them as opportunities to promote and grow your business!

This book is a full guide to your success in business starting with zero. It takes you through the practical, emotional, physical, and mystical requirements to your success! Why mystical? I will explain that later in the book! Running alongside the text is a comic book story, a modern day allegory that graphically relates to the text.

Why a comic book story? Well firstly, it's fun, and secondly, significant psychological research has shown that images can help with memory and the retention of information.[1] The *'Problem Solving'* sections give you the cold hard facts as to how to potentially resolve problems and difficult circumstances, giving you the legal and practical weight to investigate further and hopefully resolve these issues.

So, this is a deceptively simple but powerful book. If used correctly, I believe it will help you to overcome those annoying business hurdles that are probably opportunities in disguise.

To make this even more innovative, I have created a ZERO TO SUPERHERO ® skill that can be used with Amazon's Alexa.

Alexa is a digital assistant/artificial intelligence (AI) that you can talk to. It is probably how we will interact with computers in the near future and is the very latest in voice recognition, and I'm sure this technology will be significantly developed in the future. You can ask Alexa questions about business and this book, and she will answer you! Just say:

"ALEXA, ASK ZERO SUPERHERO…"

Or, **"ALEXA, TELL ZERO SUPERHERO…"**

---

[1] Bizarre imagery as an effective memory aid: The importance of distinctiveness. McDaniel, Mark A.; Einstein, Gilles O. Journal of Experimental Psychology: Learning, Memory, and Cognition, Vol 12(1), Jan 1986, 54-65

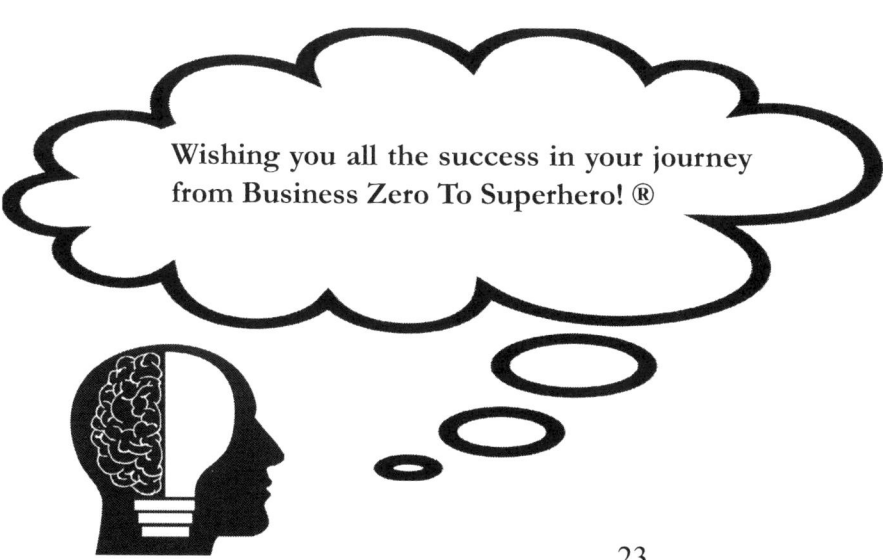

INTRODUCTION

Comic Book Page 1

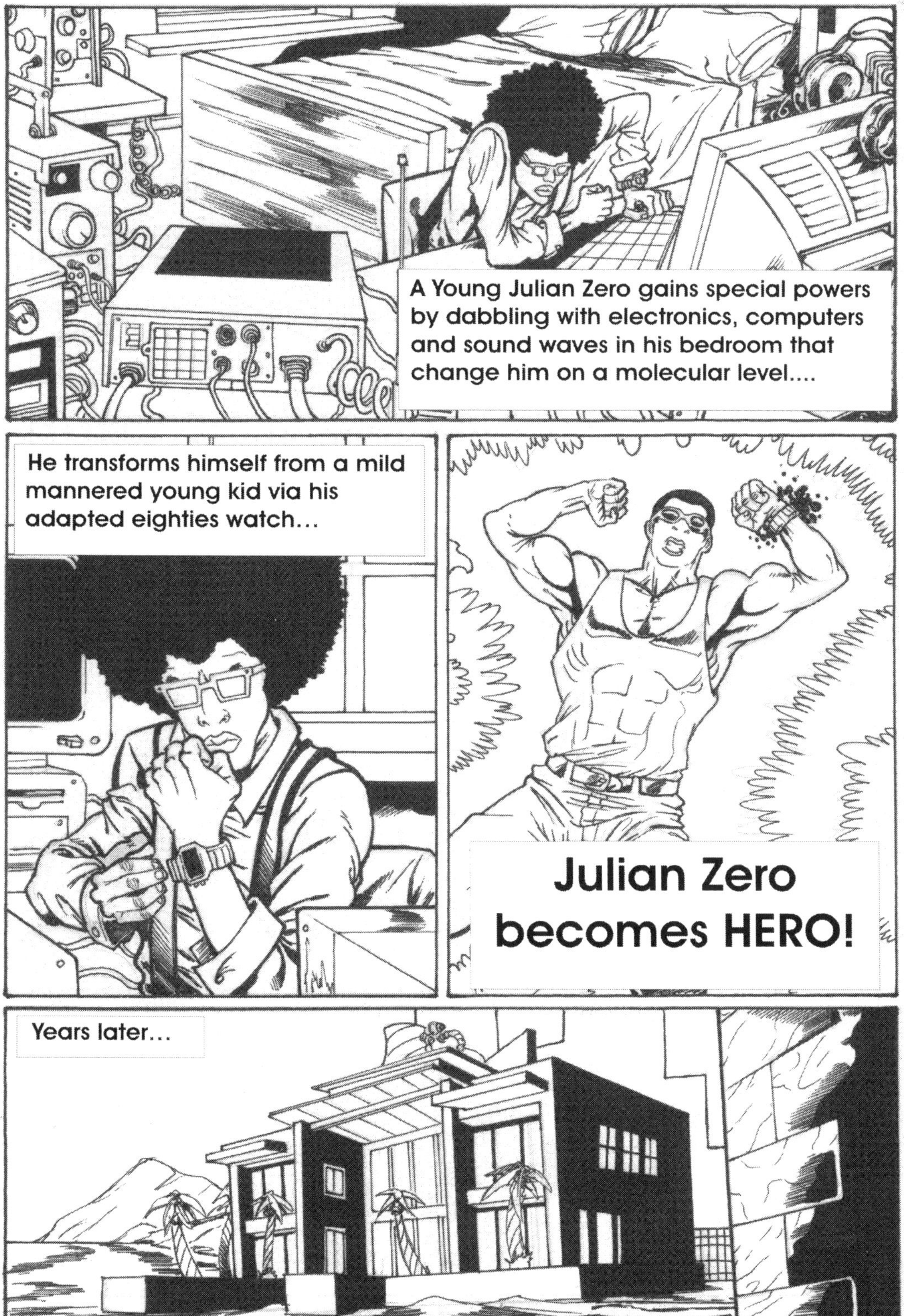

INTRODUCTION

My name is Graham Jules. My friends call me Jules, and I'm writing this book to help you make a load of money from almost nothing, wherever you come from and whatever your background.

I was born in 1968 from West Indian parents who came to England in the sixties, when signs such as 'No Dogs, No Blacks' were commonplace at hotel rooms or B&Bs. They came to England with no education, no job, in racially difficult times and somehow survived – a definite inspiration to me growing up.

As a child, things were good, but looking back, we were poor. Pocket money or annual holidays didn't exist in my family, and designer clothes, fancy shoes and trainers were definitely not on the cards for any of us. But we survived, we didn't feel poor as my parents worked hard and luckily for me, and for my brother and little sister, they managed to provide us with the essentials in life on the minimum wage they received.

My parents did their best with limited resources, and I recall my mother sitting down with us drawing pictures at a young age. They were masters at keeping us entertained with minimal outlay. As a kid I loved computers, music, and electronics, and I used to save any gifts of money from relatives at Christmas and birthdays to make small electronic circuits, such as an electronic dice and other weird gadgets. I was thrilled when my parents saved up to buy us our first computer, a Sinclair ZX81 for £69, very cheap, but a lot for my parents.

Electric Dreams

At the time, (the early eighties), computers were not as common as they are now, and my friends at school would ask, 'Why do you need a computer? What can it do?'

I didn't know then what a profound impact owning a computer at such a young age would have. I taught myself basic programming and would program small applications on our black and white TV set! Yes, I guess I was a bit of a geek at heart, but I also had a huge interest in music, and combined my early computer skills with electronics to build an electronic drum machine that could be programmed from the ZX81 computer!

I used to dream of owning a recording studio and working with sound. I even applied to the BBC but was turned down. Leaving school as a young black kid in the eighties was not easy. I sent about 100 letters out to recording studios and got two replies, both rejections! I remember being interviewed for a job in the City of London and the interviewer asked me if I thought I would fit in, as there were not many people like me in the city. I applied for all kinds of jobs but had no luck, until one day, I spotted an ad in the *Evening Standard* for a computer operator and, to my surprise, got through the application process and got myself a job (on a three-month contract) as a trainee computer operator for an American merchant bank in Southwark – result!

My first job paid £10,000 a year which was an absolute fortune to my family, and I was earning several thousand more than my dad! Life as a computer operator was good but I dreamt of working in music. I had been in a band in my spare time and had taught myself the rudiments of guitar and bass and keyboards, and would buy bits of music equipment with my wages. I built up quite a sizeable array of recording and studio-recording gizmos. After a few years of working as a computer operator, I decided to go freelance through an agency. It was then that I set up my first limited company, with no idea really what I was doing or what a limited company was; all I knew was that I had to set this up to get the contract and to get paid!

Floppy Business

The process introduced me to the idea of running my own business without actually running one as such. The agency would get the contract with the bank or whatever, who would then contract my company to service them with computer operations for a period of time.

While working as a computer operator, one day it suddenly dawned on me that a limited company was an actual business and that I could trade and make money besides what I was making from the contracting work. As a side business I bought a load of floppy disks in bulk and advertised in the popular music magazines. I knew that all the keyboards and music equipment would use loads of floppy disks to save sounds and music sequences, and hard disks were very big and very, very expensive in the eighties. I was right and orders poured in; I had officially started my own fledgling business aged 21!

The disk business grew and grew until hard disks became cheaper and the floppy disk practically disappeared from the computer and music scene. So, I decided to quit the disk business and the computer contracting and set up my dream – my own recording studio. My colleagues at the computer job thought I was mad and literally fell about laughing when I told them what I was going to do, but I was determined to go ahead and set up.

I promptly set up my music equipment in the living room of the flat I shared with my brother and placed an ad in Melody Maker, a popular music newspaper, and waited for the phone to ring. Luckily it did! My first job was for an electronic band called Trans Global Underground, and Blam! Studios was born!

The studios grew and grew and I moved to dedicated premises, worked on new bands and up and coming talent, and engineered remix tracks for the likes of PJ & Duncan AKA Ant and Dec, who promptly went to the top of the UK charts with 'Let's Get Ready To Rumble'.

All Work and No Play

The long hours of studio life had taken its toll, I was living with my then partner and in order to keep money coming in and to stay afloat, I was working a six to seven-day week.

The relationship did not last and we broke up very acrimoniously. After the break up, I was sleeping on couches and trying to run a business; the business was OK but seemed to be going nowhere. I was stuck working long hours for less and less money every year. I knew in my heart I had to do more to survive, but had no idea what! The studio business was great fun, but I needed a way to boost things and get some real money coming in.

One day a client came in. A young guitarist, I think. He had just finished his recording session and his dad had arrived to pick him up. The father introduced himself and said, 'You know, when I was young, I was into music and played guitar, but I gave it up.'

'Why?' I said, slightly surprised.

He replied, 'I wanted to make some real money, so I'm in property now.'

His words seemed to resonate in my mind and I knew at that moment I had found the answer. (But had no idea how I could do it, or more importantly, afford it!)

Surprise, Surprise

As it happened, the space I rented for the studio had ten units or rooms, of which I occupied three. The landlords had practically given up on running the units and most of them remained unoccupied for most of the time. One day, it suddenly dawned on me: couldn't I take over the whole building? And rent out the empty units myself? I set about approaching the landlords with my offer.

To my surprise, the landlords accepted my offer of taking over the whole building at increased rent, signed the agreement and handed over the keys for the ten units. I couldn't believe it, I was officially a landlord. I promptly set about tidying up the premises and renting them out and it all went well until one day, I had a knock on the door from the council, who said the previous landlord had not paid the business rates and as the current tenant and landlord, I was liable for £16,000 worth of business rates! SH*T! No wonder the landlords were so keen to agree to my terms!

Even though I had a huge outstanding debt to the council, I worked out an agreement with them, contacted the Valuation Office and got them to officially split the building into ten separate units. What this meant was that each unit would be liable for their own business rates, and as a landlord, I could pass this smaller liability on to the future tenants and ease myself of this massive burden. The plan worked, and slowly I filled the units and decreased the liability. But, this experience had taught me a lesson: I needed my own property in order to have real security.

Hot Property

I saved every bit I could from the units' rental and my studio business, and managed to save enough for a deposit on a small one-bedroom flat with a garden, and approached a broker to get a mortgage as since I was self-employed, no high street banks would touch me. I was successful in my application and was soon to be the proud owner of a property in South Tottenham! Not glamorous, but at least I was on the ladder. I soon let out the property and set about saving for my second property. My broker at the time informed me that he could get me finance for a £1million buy-to-let portfolio; credit was so easy to come by. Somehow that didn't feel right, so I declined his offer, but continued with purchasing another one-bed in south east London.

Incidentally, while I was buying property and letting out units, I was living in a tiny rented studio flat in Shepherds Bush and decided my next purchase would be one for me to live in. I thought I would change brokers and would get a nice property in the Docklands, east London, which was very up and coming at the time. I found a great property, the broker arranged the mortgage, and it was all systems go. Then, disaster! For some reason, the mortgage company had withdrawn the offer and the deal was going to fall through, but the broker found one last option for self-employed applicants –a company that specialised in the self-employed. It sounded reasonable; I signed on the dotted line. This was the start of a big mistake on my part.

DISASTER, DARLING

Comic Book Page 2

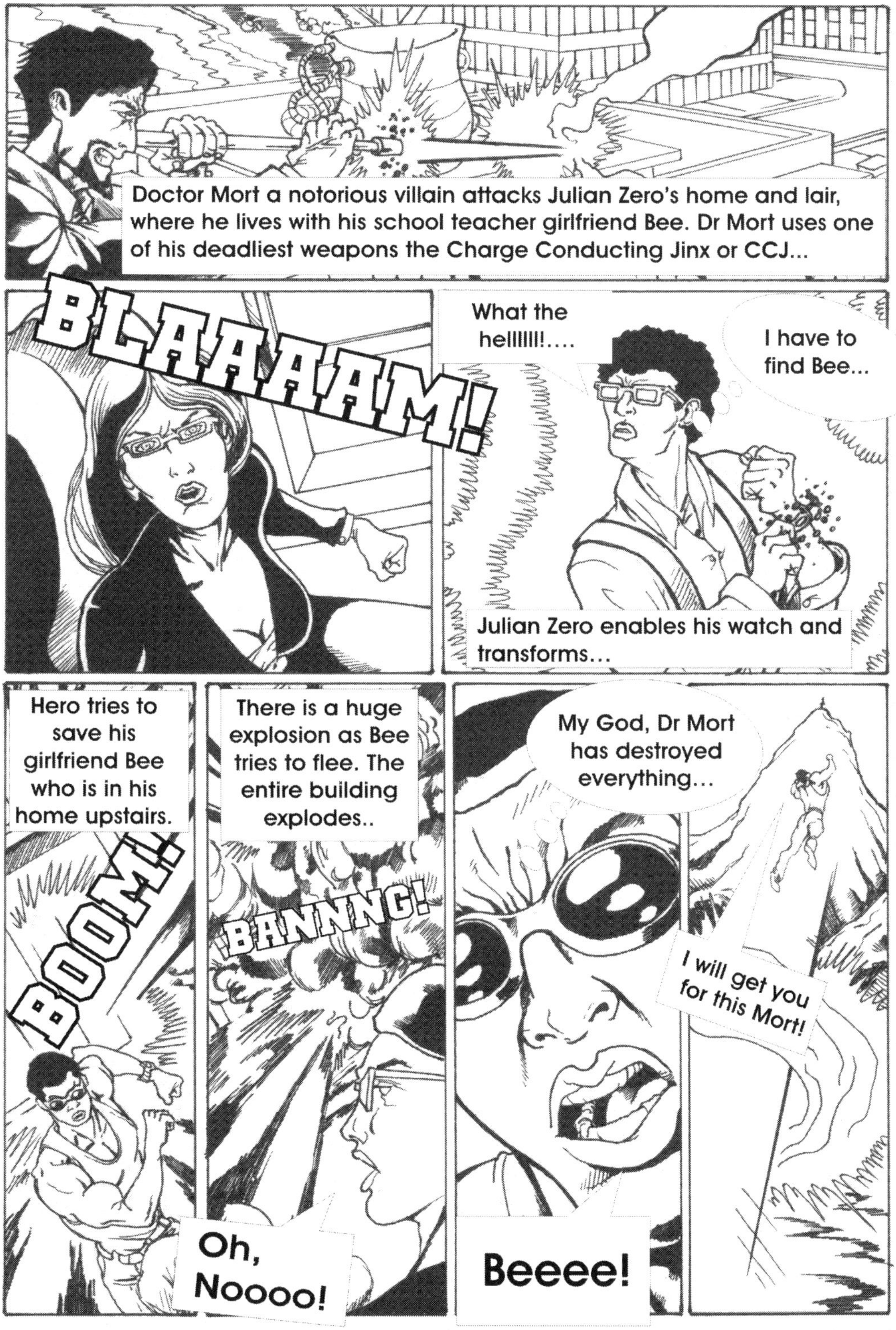

Disaster Darling

For the first couple of years, things were good. I was in a great position, I had three properties, my studio business AND my units business, things were looking good. But, beneath the surface, they were not so. The introductory period for the Docklands property was coming to an end, and I knew I had to re-mortgage to get a better interest rate. I had gone through this process successfully before with the other properties and saw no reason why I couldn't do so this time.

I was wrong – the valuation for the Docklands premises was not as high as expected and the property market was slightly faltering. I couldn't, no matter how hard I tried, shake off the increasingly expensive monthly mortgage payments.

I was haemorrhaging money each month and just about coping when one day, I got a call from the landlords at the units, stating that the lease was coming to an end and that they wanted £50,000 to renew it. There was no way I had that kind of cash available and had no option to re-mortgage. The units business collapsed and as a result, I had little income to pay the increasingly large interest payments on the Docklands property and huge arrears built up. My studio business suffered and the landlord impounded all the music equipment in lieu of payment. My then girlfriend, who I was living with, left, and I found myself alone in a two-bedroom flat facing the prospect of looming repossession. My other two properties were also in arrears, and I was forced to sell them all to try to pay off some debts and limit the damage. In the meantime, I had run up huge credit card debts trying to keep up with the bills, the mortgage, and the business, and it all just came crashing down.

Comic Book Page 3

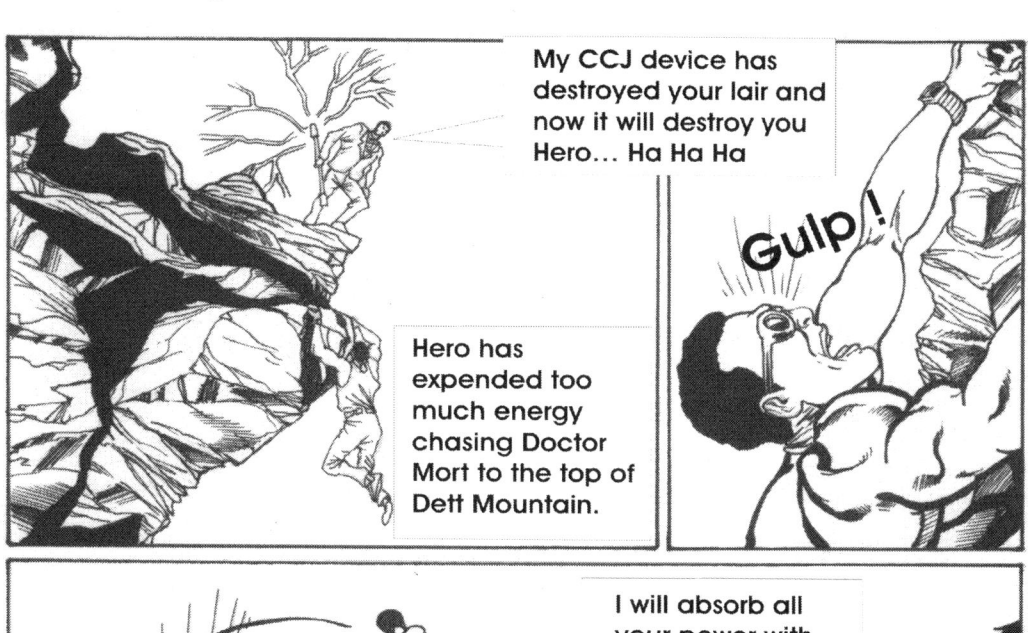

Business Zero

One day I was alone in the Docklands flat and broke down; I couldn't take it anymore. The next thing I knew, I was in hospital – a wreck, a broken man.

I had broken down and somehow managed to dial my parents who thankfully called an ambulance. My life was in tatters:

I was ill
I had no partner
I had no business
I had no home
I had no job
I had no money
and I had huge debts.

What would I do?
How would I survive?
How could I build myself up again?

This book is a guide as to how I did it, and how you can do it too – from Business Zero to Superhero ®.

STARTING OUT

Starting out from scratch (zero) is agonising. It is the most difficult place to be. Often, you have little or no idea what you want to do or how to do it. I knew I had to change my path, but had no idea where to begin. I had spent 15 years in the recording business and suddenly found myself unemployed and broke – what could I do? I had no idea, but I knew something had to change. In this book, I am going to lay out practical advice from my own experience on how to build your business from scratch. Zero. Rock bottom. It's not easy, but the first step is recognising something needs to change.

That sounds quite simple, but it is important. Often, it takes a life-changing moment; a birth, a death, or a near-death experience for us to recognise that we need to change in order to achieve our goals. We must want to change deep down or the change will never happen. Do you really want it? (Success?)

Problem Solving:

The first step to starting is stopping, (the rot, that is). Looking at the problems encountered previously:

Business Rates: If you occupy any business premises you could be liable for business rates. The amount you pay will depend on the 'rateable value' of the premises. You can find the rateable value for your premises on the Valuation Office website.[2] Your valuation is not the amount you will pay. You will usually pay around 40% of this figure annually. These bills can be several thousands of pounds a year.

However: You can claim for Small Business Rate Relief[3]. At the time of writing, up to 100% relief can be obtained for properties with a low rateable value below a certain threshold. You can also apply to the Valuation Office to re-value your property; this can be useful if you have areas that are not used for your main business (i.e., storage). Re-valuing your premises can sometimes **significantly reduce or eliminate entirely your business rate liability.**

---

[2] https://www.tax.service.gov.uk/view-my-valuation/search
[3] The Non-Domestic Rating (Small Business Rate Relief) (England) Order 2012

Repossession: The mortgage company has a right to exercise a power of sale on the property if you are two months in arrears on interest paid on a residential mortgage, or if you are in breach of the mortgage deed.[4] There is also a right to possession on breach of a mortgage term.

However: An application by a mortgage company for possession may be suspended or postponed by the court if you can show that you can pay the arrears.[5] Most importantly, this could mean just the missed payments, not the entire mortgage balance. Basically, do not ignore the situation. Turn up to court and put forward a payment plan for the arrears. If you can show that you can pay within a 'reasonable' amount of time, you can probably save your home. What is reasonable? Well, there is no definition, so it is up to you to argue the length of time you suggest is reasonable.

Commercial lease renewals. You may have a right to renew: Commercial tenancies that fall within the Landlord and Tenant Act 1954 have a right to renew. This means the landlord must give you a new contract at the end of the lease. If you want to protect your security of tenure, you need to apply to the court before your existing lease expires. It is up to you to negotiate the new rental payments with the landlord.

---

[4] s103 Law of Property Act 1925
[5] s36 Administration of Justice Acts 1970

Please note, however, that the landlord can prevent renewal on grounds such as demolition or redevelopment.[6] Whether your agreement is within the Landlord and Tenant Act will depend on your agreement. If you have contracted out or have a licence, a right to renewal may not apply.

Seizing of possessions/bailiffs: Distress (seizing of possessions) was used by landlords to recover rent arrears in commercial situations. These possessions could then be sold to cover the arrears.

However: Distress has been abolished. From April 2014, the Commercial Rent Arrears and Recovery (CRAR) came into force. What this means is that conditions must be met before distress **can be carried out. Conditions such as seven days notice**[7] **to the tenant and a minimum of seven days rent arrears are stipulated.** The goods may not be taken before 6 am or after 9 pm. This new procedure gives you time to discuss the problems with the landlord and come to an effective solution.

It is important to note CRAR only applies to commercial situations. If there is residential accommodation involved even in part, the landlord cannot distress.

Consumer debt/loans/credit cards/hire purchase: You have certain rights under the Consumer Credit Act 1974 (amended 2006). Under the Act, all credit taken out by a consumer is protected (previously up to £25,000). Business debt is not covered. Under the Act, the court has the power to give you relief for 'extortionate' and unfair lending practices (e.g. Payment Protection Insurance or PPI).[8]

---

[6] s30 Landlord and Tenant Act 1925
[7] The Taking Control of Goods Regulations 2013
[8] s140A Consumer Credit Act – Unfair relationship test

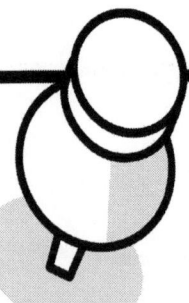

Lending agreements and documentation must be in the prescribed form, and the lender must give you notice of any arrears and any requirements to pay. If the lender fails to give notice, <u>the debtor is not liable to pay any interest, relating to the period of failure</u>. The creditor or owner shall not be entitled to enforce the agreement during the period of non-compliance.[9]

Regarding hire purchase agreements, where the loan is taken out to buy a car or other goods, these goods are protected if the borrower has paid more than one-third of the outstanding price of the goods. Therefore, the debtor shall be released from all liability under the agreement and shall be entitled to recover from the creditor <u>all sums paid by the debtor under the agreement.</u>[10] The creditor must gain 'informed' consent before they can take back the goods.

Dealing with debt problems: If you have a complaint about consumer debt or are treated unfairly, you can go to the Financial Ombudsman[11] for help. This service is amazing; they do not take sides and will try and resolve your complaint. At the time of writing the service is free, yippee!

Conclusion:

No matter how bad the situation, there are often options.

<u>Important</u>*** - Remember, this does not constitute legal advice. The law changes frequently, you should still check with your Citizens Advice Bureau or your solicitor before taking any action on matters as serious as these.

---

[9] s86D Consumer Credit Act 1974
[10] s90B Consumer Credit Act 1974
[11] http://www.financial-ombudsman.org.uk

What You Really, Really Want?

What do you want? What are your dreams? Until you know what you want, you cannot aim for it.

Do you want:
- A successful business?
- A nice car?
- A castle?
- An expensive house?
- A loving partner?

Or, all of them?

No matter how silly your dream may seem, you need to embrace it and accept it to make it real. I had to set in my mind what I wanted. I knew I wanted a successful business, a nice car, money, somewhere nice to live and a loving partner. What kind of business could give me these things?

Money, Money, Money

What type of business to choose? I get friends asking me, what is the best business to go into to make money? I say there is money in everything. If you think about it, the sofa or chair you are sitting on was sold, the TV, the bed, your breakfast cereal, your iPod, your phone, your clothes, the pictures on your wall etc, etc. The truth is, there is money in all of these businesses. The question is, which business could I make money in? I truly believe that you can only make money in a business you are passionate about. If you are into gardening, your enthusiasm and passion will show and you will draw customers. If you are into computers, you will be passionate and will love messing about with them, finding out about all of the latest models. What is your passion or interest? Business is tough. If you set up in something you are not passionate about, you will burn out or lose interest. And, even if you do make it, the money will be of no consolation, as you will be miserable!

Do not set up a business just for the money! You will fail, if not financially, then emotionally.

Once you know which field you are passionate about, the hard part is working out how to make money out of it. Not hard, I hear you say, just sell it. Simple? Not quite.

Free At Last

So, your passion lies with hairdressing. You could charge people and make money for doing their hair. If you are into computers, you could repair computers. Or, if you are into music, you could DJ at weddings. All of these businesses are great, but in my mind, you need to think carefully at this stage. Why? Here's why:

How many haircuts could you give in a day? 10? 20? 30? Just say you could give 20 haircuts at £30 each. That would mean a maximum of £600 a day, and you would need to work flat-out. It would be the same thing for the computer guy and the same thing for the DJ. That's not bad money, I hear you say. Yes, I agree, but the catch is:

If you are cutting clients' hair, fixing computers, or DJ-ing, these are skills where the clients want you to be present. They want you, your skills, your expertise, and often no one else is good enough. If you do a good job, you become a victim of your success. What this means with these types of businesses, is that you are actually setting yourself up with a 'job'. That is great, but it is important to understand the difficulties.

A job is often paid by the hour. This means that there is a maximum to the amount you can earn in a day. Often you, the business owner, need to be present all the time. This is a serious hindrance to your earning potential!

Even if you paid someone to do your highly skilled trade, would they do it to your standards? Or would your clients take to them? Would you need to spend hours training, only for them to leave for a competitor or to set up for themselves?

I set up my business in the early years as a studio engineer. Great, but I soon realised I was trapped as I couldn't leave the studio, and my life outside the studio suffered. The point for me in setting up a business is to be 'free', not to set oneself up with another job, even if you are passionate about it.

Comic Book Page 4

Julian Zero is powerless and broken. While unconscious he has a dream at the bottom of Dett Mountain....

You are powerless, you must create a time machine to defeat the evil Dr Mort...

Sleeping Beauty

So, what type of business can set you free? It's not dependent on the business or your skills, but the business should have the following qualities built in:

1) It should not be 100% reliant on your skills.

2) It should not be 100% reliant on your time.

3) It should have the potential to make money while you are asleep!

Yes! I know number three is crazy, I hear you say, but it's true. When forming your business think in your mind, how could I structure this business so I can make money while I am sleeping? If you do this, even if you burn out or get bored, you will still be making money. So this is IMPORTANT in order to make real money – for instance:

1) You're interested in hairdressing. Maybe you can design a new hair product, or a device you could sell or licence to a manufacturer who could distribute it nationally or worldwide. People would still buy and use your product while you are asleep. Criteria met!

2) You are interested in computers. You could set up a website where people could register and get tips on how to configure and repair their computer problems. Criteria met!

3) You are interested in music DJ-ing. You could create a party CD that you could distribute and sell nationally or worldwide. Criteria met!

These are just examples, but hopefully you can see the difference. All three have the potential for unlimited sales in theory, independent from your time and input, this is often called 'passive income' or 'passive residual income'.

> The truth is, your most valuable asset is time. Plan to preserve it.

Problem Solving:

What business to choose? : Just to reassure you that most business categories have the potential for success, here is some data from the Office for National Statistics[12] for businesses with turnovers of between £100,000 to £249,000.

As we can see in (12.) overleaf (Page 48), the professional scientific and technical sector have the largest number of businesses with a turnover in the range with a total of 124,835 businesses. The sector with the lowest number of businesses with a turnover in the range is (14.), Public administration and defence. Surprisingly Arts, entertainment, recreation services (17.) has 24,515 businesses with a turnover in the range while finance and insurance only have 8,505 businesses, but this can probably be explained due to high regulation in the finance sector. So, this is evidence that there are opportunities to generate substantial revenue in most industry sectors.

Conclusion:

With that in mind, there should be no reason to choose a sector just 'for the money'. The key to success in your chosen sector will always be how _you_ execute your business idea, NOT the idea itself.

---

[12] Adapted from 2015 data from the Office for National Statistics licensed under the Open Government Licence v.3.0.

**Remember
A business exists to set
you free:**

Ensure you understand the need for passive income in your business model at an early stage to ensure you maximise your earning potential and your time.

Linear income – income that requires some continuous effort on your part, often on an hourly basis.

Passive residual income – income that is separate from the number of hours worked.

Businesses With A Turnover of £100,000 to £249,000 (2015)

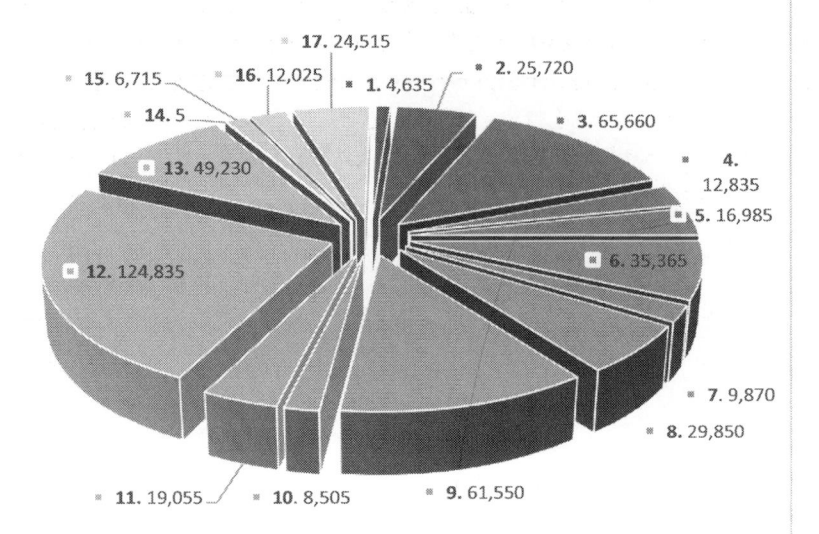

- 1. 4,635
- 2. 25,720
- 3. 65,660
- 4. 12,835
- 5. 16,985
- 6. 35,365
- 7. 9,870
- 8. 29,850
- 9. 61,550
- 10. 8,505
- 11. 19,055
- 12. 124,835
- 13. 49,230
- 14. 5
- 15. 6,715
- 16. 12,025
- 17. 24,515

- 1. Forestry & fishing
- 2. Production
- 3. Construction
- 4. Motor trades
- 5. Wholesale
- 6. Retail
- 7. Transport & Storage (inc. postal)
- 8. Accommodation & food services
- 9. Information & communication
- 10. Finance & insurance
- 11. Property
- 12. Professional, scientific & technical
- 13. Business administration & support services
- 14. Public administration & defence
- 15. Education
- 16. Health
- 17. Arts, entertainment, recreation & other services

Two's Company

Anyone can start trading and just place any income into their personal account; this is what is known as a sole trader. The problem with that is that you are taxed on all of your income after allowable expenses, and you pay National Insurance on these earnings. You will also have to register with HMRC as self-employed. However, if you set up as a limited company, the company is treated as a separate entity. So, there are in effect two entities involved; yourself (the director), and the business entity. Tax-wise, you are taxed separately from your business. Your limited company will only be taxed on its profits and the company will not pay National Insurance on those earnings. Big difference!

A limited company, however, will be required by law to file accounts with Companies House once a year and also file other documents such as annual returns, so you will need an accountant. If you are late filing, the fines can amount to several hundreds of pounds.

So what is best, sole trader or a limited company? Well, initially, the limited company is more expensive to run. You need to hire an accountant, pay filing fees, etc. But the savings you will make tax-wise when your company takes off will more than offset the expense. Also, looking forward, if you wish to raise money via investors, they will only invest in a limited company, not sole traders, as that is the easiest way to claim a stake legally in your business.

So, in the long run, if you are planning to grow the company, a limited company is probably the best. An added advantage of a limited company is that it separates your personal income/expenses from your business. This can save you all kinds of problems with tax, benefits, credit, and debts in the future. If you were to trade as a limited company and your company were to go bust, only the assets of the business can be seized, not your personal assets. As a sole trader, your personal possessions could be at risk.

A limited company has a certain amount of protection. They are easy to set up and can cost as little as £40 from any company formation website. You will get a Certificate of Incorporation (a kind of birth certificate for your company) and other legal documents. You need to keep them in a safe place, as you will need these to set up your limited company bank accounts.

Problem Solving:

The idea of limited liability and the implications: As discussed earlier, when you form a company (incorporate it), it is classed as a separate legal entity. This was established in legal terms in 1896 in a case called Salomon v Salomon.[13] In this case, the Director, Salomon, legally avoided personal liability for the debts of the company. What this means is as Director of the company you are not liable for the debts of the company. Therefore, if your business is sued, <u>it is the business that is sued, not you as the Director.</u> Contrast that with a sole trader business where you can be sued, and your assets claimed as an individual. The main exception to this is if there is evidence of fraud.[14] In this case, the courts may look behind the limited liability of an incorporated body. Of course, most lenders will insist on a personal guarantee from directors to ensure payment of debts should the company go belly up.

Duties of a Director: As a Director of a limited company, you have significant duties. The duties of the Director are laid out in the Companies Act.[15] A director can be held liable for failure to file accounts and other documents at Companies House. If you file late, there are penalties (£150-£1500).[16] Also, it is important to note that late filing may also give rise to personal liability for the Directors and is a <u>criminal offence</u>.[17] Ensure accounts are filed on time to avoid any problems.

---

[13] Salomon v Salomon & Co Ltd <u>[1896] UKHL</u>
[14] Gilford Motor Co Ltd v Horne [1933] Ch 935
[15] s170-s177 Companies Act 2006
financial questions and giving advice on tax, so don't just go for the cheapest.
[16] The Companies (Late Filing Penalties) and Limited Liability Partnerships (Filing Periods and Late Filing Penalties) Regulations 2008
[17] section 451 Companies Act 2006

Forming a Company, Step 1:

Choose an accountant. (Yes, this really is the first step!)

Choosing an accountant: Choosing an accountant is not difficult, but fees vary greatly, so shop around. Personally, I do not think it is worth the risk to use software and attempt to do this yourself (unless of course, you are an accountant). Ensure your accountant is qualified with a recognised body. (CIMA, ICAEW, ICAS, ACCA).[18] There are many accountancy firms that specialise in small businesses, so expect to pay £40-£60 a month initially. Most charge more as your turnover and complexity of the business grow. Bear in mind that a good friendly accountant can really help your business grow by answering your financial questions.

Forming a Company, Step 2:

Get a registered office company address.

To set up a limited company, you will need a registered office address. The registered office is where all official correspondence will be served. Even as a sole trader, it is probably a good idea to have a separate mailing address. You could use your home address, but this would mean your home address would appear in the public record and would be available to customers. Many accountants provide a registered office service for a fee. This makes sense as usually, it is the accountant who would need these documents in any case. However, there are many companies that provide this service for around £50 annually. Just do an online search for 'registered office address'. You can then collect or have the mail forwarded to you.

---

[18] Chartered Institute of Management Accountants, Institute of Chartered Accountants, Association of Chartered Certified Accountants.

Forming a Company Step 3:

Choose whether you are going to be a limited company or sole trader.

Setting up a Limited Company: If you are setting up as a limited company, you need to get your company formed and registered. You need to choose a name and approach a company formation agent who will fill in the relevant paperwork and file it with Companies House for a fee. Do a search for 'limited company formation' online, and you will see there are plenty of companies offering this service for tens of pounds. Ensure you choose a name that makes you stand out from the pack. You cannot register a name if it exists already or is defamatory.[19]

Setting up as a sole trader: If you are setting up as a sole trader you need to inform HMRC (Tax office) by going to:
https://online.hmrc.gov.uk/registration/newbusiness/introduction

Forming a Company, Step 4:

Set up a bank account.

Setting up your Bank Account:

Choosing a bank for your business used to involve a walk down the high street, probably to your high street personal provider, but not anymore. You may want to consider opening your business banking to an entirely different provider. It is not widely known that banks can take from one account to pay another (Setting-off).[20] So, if things go wrong and your personal account is with the same provider, you may find that account is debited without warning. (This is more likely for a sole trader than a limited company due to the separate legal entity reasons mentioned earlier). The flipside is that your current provider will have a full history of your financial dealings, so in theory, you will be more likely to be accepted for any business products you apply for.

---

[19] s53 Companies Act 2006
[20] http://www.financial-ombudsman.org.uk/publications/ombudsman-news/40/40_setoff.htm

Increased competition in the banking sector has meant there are numerous options. In 2013, the Chancellor of the Exchequer created the Business Banking Insight (BBI), to give small businesses an impartial indication of customer satisfaction of banking providers. http://www.businessbankinginsight.co.uk/ . Choose a bank that is convenient for your business; look at options such as free banking for start-ups.

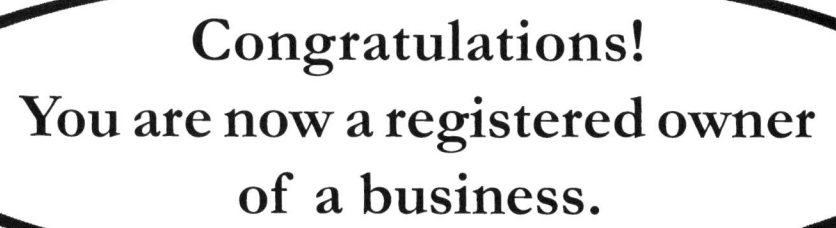

Congratulations! You are now a registered owner of a business.

Tax implications:

Don't be tempted to ignore the tax implications of setting up a business.

Tax and a Limited Company

If you have set up a limited company, your company will be charged corporation tax on its profits. (Currently 19% - 2018)[21]. Understand that profit is different to revenue or turnover (the amount coming into the bank), therefore, if your business is not profitable, (the expenses of running the business are greater than the revenue) the company will not pay tax.

You also need to understand that if you are running a limited company, the company's earnings are not yours. Remember, you are a separate entity. Therefore, HMRC will consider you an owner and employee of the business. (You are NOT self-employed). You can pay yourself a wage via Pay as You Earn (PAYE), or you can take money out of the business via dividends. (Or you can choose to take nothing at all). If you take money out under PAYE, the normal thresholds and allowances apply, so therefore, you can earn up to £11,000 per annum and pay no tax.[22] Directors of limited companies will pay National Insurance only on income over £8060, and you will need to run a payroll and inform HMRC of the monthly pay details. (Your accountant can do this for you.)

If you go down the dividend route, you can draw up to £5000 tax-free. If the dividend is higher than £5000, you can offset with your personal allowance (£11,000), and you will be charged 7.5% on the remainder up to a threshold of £32,000. You will be charged a higher rate of 32% on dividend income over the £43,000 threshold.[23]

---

[21] https://www.gov.uk/government/publications/rates-and-allowances-corporation-tax/rates-and-allowances-corporation-tax
[22] https://www.gov.uk/income-tax-rates/current-rates-and-allowances
[23] https://www.gov.uk/tax-on-dividends/how-dividends-are-taxed

Tax and a Sole Trader

If you are a sole trader (self-employed), you will need to pay income tax (20% basic rate) and Class 2 and Class 4 National Insurance contributions on your profits. Class 2 is currently £2.80 per week if your profits are over £5965, or you may pay Class 4, which is an additional 9% if your profits are £8060 or more. An additional 2% is payable if your profits are over £43,000.[24]

VAT

VAT (Value Added Tax) is a tax paid on most goods and services sold. The current rate is 20% (2018).[25] The consumer or buyer pays the 20% when they buy your goods or services, and you collect this and pay back to Customs and Excise the amount of VAT you can claim back from your purchases. Both self-employed and limited companies must register for VAT if their turnover is over £85,000.[26] You can choose to register below the threshold, for instance, if you want to claim back the VAT on your start-up costs. You must then file a VAT return every three months. (Your accountant can do this for you.)

---

[24] https://www.gov.uk/self-employed-national-insurance-rates
[25] https://www.gov.uk/vat-rates
[26] https://www.gov.uk/vat-registration-thresholds

Conclusion:

(Phew)! So there you have it, at first glance, the limited company appears more advantageous, but which method you choose to pay yourself will depend on your personal circumstances. As you can see, there are quite a few tax implications and statutory duties to forming a company. Therefore, the need for an accountant <u>first</u> to discuss and sort these issues for you is important and can save you from all kinds of horrible issues later.

START UP COSTS

Money's Too Tight To Mention

So, you have in your mind the business model that will set you free. But how can we start? It's going to cost money! And we have zero – or very little. What to do?

In my mind, it's often easy to use money as an excuse for not doing something! We often say for example:

'If only I had more money, I would exercise more and go to the gym.'

Or, 'If I had more money, I would start my own business'.

Or, 'If I had more money, I would be happier'.

Yes, there is an element of truth in these, but for me, money is not the problem, it is the ideas.

If you had an idea how to exercise properly, you would exercise at home and be fitter.

If you had an idea how to start a business, you would start one.

If you had an idea of what makes you happy, you would be happy.

If you had an idea of how to get money, you would get it!

Money is a tool. In our modern society, marketing men who want us to buy products and services tell us that unless we buy into these products or services, we cannot possibly begin our lives and be fulfilled – wrong!

So how do we get hold of the money for our business start-up without robbing a bank? Well, there are a few ways, some obvious, some not so, and some risky:

Dirty Cash

1) **Loans:** Bank loans.

2) **Credit unions:** Your local credit union may help with low-cost finance for your venture even if you've had problems.

Loans are great, but the big downside is that you have to pay them back! You will often need good credit or they will be difficult or very expensive to come by.

3) **Jobs:** Stay in your job if you have one, or get one and fund the business from that until it is self-sustaining. The plus side is that you can support yourself with your job until the business grows. The downside, time spent on your business will be minimised.

4) **Grants:** Grants are fantastic; you don't have to pay them back! The downside is that they are very difficult to come by.

5) **CDFIs:** Community development finance institutions. These bodies often offer low-cost business loans.

6) **Sell stuff:** If you cannot get credit, or have no access to grants, you can always sell, sell, sell! With a website such as eBay, you can sell all of your old stuff you don't use anymore and pocket a nice sum for your start-up.

7) **The government:** If you have none of the above or are on a low income, your local council or benefits office may be able to help you set up – ask!

8) **Crowd funding:** A relatively new way to raise finance on the internet. The way it works is a large number of individuals invest in your company at small values from a few pounds to several thousand until you reach your funding target. The pro is, it's not a loan so you won't have monthly payments. The downside, you may end up with 200 small shareholders in your company and have to give away a large stake in your business.

9) **Private investors:** Get someone to invest in your business and cough up the funds. The downside is that they will want a percentage of the business.

Family and friends are often a good place to start at this stage (also, see chapter entitled 'How To Find Angel Investors').

10) **Investments:** If you have some cash, you could try investing it in say, stocks and shares, and grow your cash over time and use any gains towards your start-up. This is risky, however. Although, if you read up about it and are careful, it's possible to make money. Be careful not to put all of your cash into the investment in order to win 'big'.

11) **Events:** Hold an event or launch party and charge at the door. If you promote it right, your launch event could fund the start of the business!

> If you have no money at all, this is the hard part. You may need to go through several of the previous steps until you accumulate enough funds to start.
> Remember to launch early and as cheaply as possible. Don't give up. You now have an idea how to get the money and eventually you will get it!

Comic Book Page 5

Julian Zero sets up a make shift lab in the city and tries desperately with limited resources to get the right components for his time machine.

He scourers junk yards for parts...

"I must source components for the time machine."

"The algorithms just will not work.."

His computer systems are not working correctly...

Julian Zero bangs the table frustrated.

Bang!

The time machine springs to life.

Wirrrrrrrr!

"I am yourself from an alternate reality. My name is Unlimited Hero!"

"My God... I need your help, help me complete the time machine.."

60

Problem Solving:

Here, I will give a brief review of solutions that could help you get that initial funding. I am not endorsing any of these but expressing my personal opinion as to what I believe is achievable from my own experience. (I have contacted and or experienced the services of these providers first-hand.)

Bank Loans:

Santander.

Pros: - They will loan up to £25,000 unsecured to small businesses, with no business plan. Financing within two weeks is possible.

Cons: – This bank says they want to help small businesses, but if you are looking for funding here you will need a 'Good' credit score (See later in the chapter about credit scores) and some kind of trading history, usually two years. This bank, like all major banks, is a slave to their lending algorithm. It's not impossible to get decent funding from them, but you will need to get all your ducks in a row first, (see later chapters on improving your credit). However, if you own a property, most banks will not have a problem lending to you.

Barclays Bank.

Pros: - This bank is more concerned with what you are planning and how you are going to achieve it. They can lend up to £25,000 unsecured.

Cons: – You will need to supply a business plan, cash flow forecast, profit and loss, trading accounts, and have a good credit score.

Metro Bank.

Pros: - This bank is a relatively new player bank that says it can help small businesses with a loan up to £25,000 unsecured

Cons: - However, the small print does suggest security will be required in some cases.

All the other 'high street' banks offer a variation of up to £25,000. Some need security; some need business plans, some don't. Most will require that you bank with them to access other services such as overdrafts and credit cards.

Barclays Corporate Card.[27]

The one exception I have found to this is Barclays, who do a corporate card that can be applied for by customers of other banks. However, you do need a turnover of at least £10,000 a year before you can apply. Since this is a corporate card, it should not appear on your personal credit file but on your businesses. (More on that later.)

Bank Business Overdrafts.

Most banks offer business overdraft facilities

Pros: - Lending criteria may be less strict than getting a bank loan. You will only pay for the amount you are overdrawn.

Cons: - You will more than likely have to be a customer of the bank to get this facility. The bank can withdraw the facility at any time and ask for the balance to be paid in full. Overdrafts can be expensive interest wise.

---

[27] https://www.barclaycard.co.uk/business/making- payments/business-credit-cards

Peer To Peer Lenders:

Next, you can go to peer to peer lenders for your funds.

These lenders are alternatives to the high street banks and some are funded by individuals who lend a fraction of your loan. So, it is possible that five hundred people could lend you ten pounds each at a very good interest rate. All of these peer to peer lending firms declare that they exist only to help small businesses. Do not believe them, it is a huge industry that is returning huge profits for the main players; they still will not give away money without certain criteria being met.

Funding Circle.[28]

Pros: - These guys give good interest rates on loans. They do not have such a strict algorithm as the high street banks. You can usually get funds within a week. They give a loan that will appear on your business credit file if you are a limited company. The initial application will not hurt your credit file.

Cons: - Since they cater for your loan manually. You may not get the amount you are seeking, but a significantly smaller amount.

---

[28] https://www.fundingcircle.com/uk/

RateSetter.[29]

Pros: - These guys also give good interest rates, sometimes much cheaper than the high street.

Cons: - However, their lending algorithm appears to be on par with or maybe even stricter than some of the main high street banks, so you will probably need very good credit to be successful here.

Capital On Tap.[30]

Pros: - Say they can offer up to £25,000 to small businesses at competitive rates. They say they can fund a business within 2 hours of completion.

Cons: - The business will need at least £24,000 of turnover before you can apply.

Crowdcube.[31]

Pros: - Not a loan but an investment from the crowd, so you don't have a monthly payment. No turnover requirements.

Cons: - Whether you get funding or not is at the whim of the crowd. There is no set criteria, so you may not get the funds you are looking for despite the viability of your proposal or business. If you are successful, it may be a pain dealing with multiple investors. You will have to provide a business plan to investors, and your investment proposal may also be visible to the public and your competitors.

Fair Business Loans.[32]

Pros: - These guys can give up to £50,000 funding to small businesses unsecured. They do not use a strict algorithm.

---

[29] https://www.ratesetter.com/
[30] https://www.capitalontap.com
[31] https://www.crowdcube.com/
[32] https://www.fairfinance.org.uk/business-loans

Cons: - You will more than likely need to have some trading history. Since they do not have a strict algorithm, you may be offered significantly less than you applied for.

The Government - Start Up Loans Scheme[33] and British Business Bank[34].

Pros: - You can get up to £25,000 pounds unsecured. No strict lending criteria. Set up specifically for start-up businesses. You get a business mentor. Great if you have little or no credit history. Once you are more established, growth funds may be available.

Cons: - May take a long time to get funding (Up to 3 months). No indication as to how many businesses actually achieve £25,000 funding. The loan will appear on your personal credit file, and as such may hinder other finance applications you may need personally.

Short Term Small Business Lenders.

These lenders may be useful if you just need short term funding.

Iwoca.[35]

Pros: - These guys can operate very quickly and give you an approved overdraft that you can dip into (drawdown), and pay back as and when. You also get your own relationship manager.

Cons: - Their overdraft facility is not guaranteed and can be taken away at any time, so do not rely on it being there when you need it. You will need to pay back between 6-12 months. Their rates are not the cheapest. Subsequent applications can be hit and miss. The relationship manager is a good idea but in practice does not work since they often do not return calls/enquiries.

---

[33] https://www.startuploans.co.uk
[34] http://british-business-bank.co.uk/
[35] https://www.iwoca.co.uk/

Fleximize.[36]

Pros: - These can give short-term funding between 6-24 months. They say they do not follow strict criteria for their lending.

Cons: - They do follow strict criteria for their lending. You will probably need a good to very good credit score to be successful here.

Funding Brokers

These may help you access lenders that are less well known on the market, but beware of upfront fees.

Funding Exchange. [37]

Genie Lending. [38]

Boost Capital. [39]

Conclusion:

Not an exhaustive list, but this should be enough to get you researching. As a start-up, you are caught in a difficult position. You need funding, but most lenders require a trading history to lend, catch 22. Before you apply for any funding, it is essential you verify your credit file. You may also need to 'bootstrap' (start your company with your own limited funds), to show you have a viable business to potential lenders. If you happen to own property, most lenders can fund you with a secured loan on your property, obviously, this is risky, so you will need to think carefully before going down that route.

---

[36] https://fleximize.com/
[37] https://www.fundingxchange.co.uk/
[38] http://www.genielending.co.uk/
[39] https://www.boostcapital.co.uk/

Computer Says No

OK, so now you have the ideas, but what if your credit is in a bad way and your options are limited? Well, I'm going to tell you how to get credit AND how to improve it!

Remember, it is not essential that you borrow money to start your business; as we've shown above, you could start by funding your business upfront by bootstrapping. But sometimes it is essential, as you need a large amount to begin or you need capital to tide you over until you get paid from your clients. I would recommend you do as much as you can with your business model to minimise the credit you take on and limit what credit you give to others. Get paid as quickly as possible. That way, your cash can be used to grow the business rather than lying in the pockets of bad payers.

It amazes me how little people know about credit and how it works. The phrase people use is, 'I'm on a blacklist, I can't get credit'. The truth is, there is no such thing as a blacklist, but there is a thing called a credit file. The good news is that almost everyone can improve their credit file. The downside is that it may take plenty of time depending on how bad your credit is.

If you are finding it impossible to get credit or cannot get the credit you want, the first step is to get your credit file. You can get your credit file from credit reference agencies such as Equifax or Experian. It will cost you a couple of quid to get your file.

When you take out credit, the finance company will tell the credit reference agencies who will keep a record of all your payments and history. If you fail to pay back a loan or credit card, this will also show on your file. It is very important to remember that your phone bill – landline or mobile – will also appear on your credit file, as well as your internet access. The credit reference agencies will keep records for 6–12 months for any financial agreements, and six years for any defaults or County Court Judgements. (A judgement will be made if you fail to pay and the loan company takes you to court.)

As an additional note, do not waste valuable funds on companies offering services to repair your credit file. You can do it yourself for almost zero!

Credit Where Credit Is Due

Things to note to improve your credit:

1) If you have very bad credit, after six years, your file will be wiped clean completely! (Even if you have paid nothing back!)

2) If you can keep regular payments on time for 6 –12 months, your credit file will be improved despite any previous history. NEVER make a late payment or miss a payment.

3) If you live with someone, i.e. shared accommodation, check their file does not appear on yours. The credit reference agency may have linked you if they believe you are financially linked. If you are not linked, you can remove any bad entries by writing to the agency.

4) Ensure you are on the electoral roll as this will hugely affect your file. You can join by contacting your local council.

5) Ensure you take out *some* credit. Having no credit on your file at all is not a good thing, as it shows you have no history, so get some to improve your rating. Don't go mad, get a phone line, a mobile contract or a credit card with a low balance, and pay it off on time and stay within the limit, and within 6 –12 months, your credit rating will improve.

7) Stay at your address for three years or more. Credit agencies like people who stay put. Do not move unnecessarily.

8) Get a current account with a high street bank if you do not have one. Get a chequebook or debit card if at all possible.

9) Do not give false information on your credit applications. Any false information will be flagged up in your file.

10) Do not apply for loads of credit at once if you get rejected, leave it for three to six months and try again. Applying for loads of credit will have a negative impact on your credit rating.

11) If you are declared bankrupt, your bankruptcy will be dismissed after one year, after which, you are free to build your credit and enter into credit agreements again! (A record will be kept on your credit file for 6 years.)

So ALL situations are solvable given enough time!

Once you have improved your credit using the techniques mentioned, just take out additional credit agreements ensuring you pay them on time. If you are clever about this, your credit file will improve significantly within 6–12 months.

Resist the temptation to go mad and start a spending spree with your newly found credit. Once improved, keep an eye on your file to ensure it stays healthy. Remember, you are building your credit file to be 'free', not to be tied to huge bills! Remember, I've been there!

Virtual Insanity

Remember, if you set up a limited company, that company will be treated as a separate 'entity' or person. Imagine it as a virtual person that you control! Therefore, you will also need to build the credit file for your new virtual 'friend' (your business), AND yourself. You can avoid problems later by separating your business and personal finances from the outset and keeping an eye on both credit files.

To build your business credit file, just open a credit account with a supplier that reports to the credit reference agencies – a mobile phone contract or stationery supplier, for example.

Ensure you start the account in the full company name, not your own name, and if possible, have a separate registered office address for your business rather than your home address to avoid all confusion. (Registered office addresses can be hired for a few pounds a month.)

Just ensure you pay on time and your limited company credit rating will improve over time. Once improved, you can apply for additional credit agreements, such as charge cards, credit cards, and loans. But remember, your credit file is like gold; it's very precious, so treat it as such.

> **If you get into difficulties the same rules apply as personal credit. Any defaults, CCJs (County Court Judgements) etc. will stay on your company file for six years.**

Laughing On Judgement Day

As mentioned above, County Court Judgements are made in the courts and are applied to your credit file by the credit reference agencies. You will get these if there is a dispute and you fail to pay. These will stay on your file for up to six years, so it is important that you avoid these at all costs. If you already have a CCJ, all may not be lost:

1) You can pay the judgement amount and have the court and credit reference agency mark it as 'satisfied'. Although it will still stay on your file, it will be marked as paid and will not affect your credit rating as much.

2) If the CCJ is incorrect or you were not served any papers, or you have paid the amount prior to the original hearing, you can apply to 'set aside' the judgement for a fee (around £80) with an N244 form. What this means is that the court will hear your case and if successful, the CCJ will be removed from the record completely! The claim will then start from the beginning again, so it may not be over completely, but you will have another opportunity to pay or state your case at a hearing.

Be warned though, do not lie to get judgements set aside. You must have a valid reason; you could be prosecuted or jailed if you use this fraudulently.

Problem Solving:

Remember, your credit score is just an indication to the lender of your financial standing, and it attempts to forecast your likelihood of repayment. Different credit reference agencies will have different scores. Having a good credit score does not guarantee that you will get funding. Lenders take into account other factors, such as affordability, so it is important to be able to show the funding is affordable as well as having a good credit score.

To further complicate matters, each lender has its own methods for scoring, so your high score may be successful with one provider, but you may be rejected by another. Lenders are often looking for a particular profile for new businesses. Some prefer high-risk, others the reverse. Having said that, most finance is now scored by a computer algorithm, so a high score will give you a pretty good indication of your chances.

What is a good score? It depends, 700 + is deemed as fair to good with Experian, while 400 + is deemed as good with Equifax.

Steps to fix or turbo-charge your credit file and credit score.

Turbo-charge Your Credit Step 1:

Register for an online credit report service.

You need to gain access to your credit file. As discussed previously, you can get your report for a couple of pounds from the credit reference agencies (CRA's). However, in order to turbo-charge your credit, you need more than just a snapshot of what your credit file is today. I would highly recommend you register for an online credit report service. You will then be able to log in and view your report whenever you want. This will enable you to time your credit applications and enable you to chart your progress in strengthening your file.

The problem you have is there are three main credit report agencies in the UK and many other data providers, which one do you choose? Fortunately, I have gone through the process of using all the main players, so I will give you my opinion as to the strengths and weaknesses of each provider, In effect, I will be rating the credit rating agencies for you! As usual, this is my personal opinion, and I am not endorsing any of these.

Experian:[40]

This agency has a couple of services. It is important that you do not get them mixed up since they are slightly different.

Experian Credit Expert.[41]

Pros: - This is a comprehensive credit checking service that is regularly updated. There is also a breakdown of what is harming your credit file, what is helping your credit file, and a handy chart of your credit score. Experian is one of the largest CRA's,[42] a lot of the main funding providers use Experian as part of their lending algorithm, so this can give an excellent indication as to whether you will be successful or not.

Cons: - The service costs about £15 a month at the time of writing. All the information provided can be a bit daunting. The website can be a bit slow to load.

Experian Credit Score.

Pros: - This gives you a rundown of your credit score (a figure that takes into account your credit activity and rates you accordingly) for free.

Cons: - Since this is a free service, your score is only updated every thirty days or so. You may be making decisions based on outdated information.

---

[40] http://www.experian.co.uk/
[41] https://www.creditexpert.co.uk/
[42] UK & Ireland profit of $971m 2016 p130 Group Financial Statements https://www.experian-plc.com/media/2733/experian-ar2016.pdf

Equifax:

Pros: - This service gives you access to your credit score and report. You get timely alerts if there are changes to your file. This service is relatively cheap, from £6 to update your score and £2 for a new report. Equifax is the second largest credit reference agency, so therefore, should give a good indication as to whether you will be successful in your applications.

Cons: - The website offers little by way of analysis as to what can be done to improve your score. Although, there is a listing of relevant factors affecting your score and their status. You need to pay each time you want an update on your report or credit score.

Call Credit:[43]
Again, this provider has a paid for service and free services.

Credit Compass.

Pros: - This is a more comprehensive service much in line with the Experian Credit Expert.

Cons: - There are fees to pay, around £15 per month. Call Credit is the least used credit reference agency by lenders, so the information will give you a fair indication of whether you will be successful in any applications.

Noddle.

Pros: - Call Credit's free service, Easy to use and gives you a simple indication of your score. Free for life.

Cons: - Does not appear to update your score in line with improvements in your credit activity. May not give a true indication as to how other lenders will view you.

---

[43] https://www.creditcompass.co.uk/

Other Third Party Providers

Checkmyfile.

Pros:- A product that gives you an insight into information from all the credit reference agencies. Free for thirty days. Loads of information and graphs with some analysis.

Cons: - May not give a true indication as to how lenders will view you. Data from other agencies is historical, therefore, you may make decisions based on old data.

Clearscore.

Pros: - Professes to help you build your credit. Free credit scores.

Cons: - Relatively new player in the field.

Decisions, decisions. For starters, if your credit is not great, I would go for one of the free providers since regular updating will not be necessary until you have improved your credit somewhat. If you have no major blemishes but want to improve, I would go for the Experian Credit Expert Account- this is a paid for service but it gives you comprehensive guidance and accurate information from the largest provider in the field.

Turbo-charge Your Credit, Step 2:

Check you are on the Electoral Roll.

Once you have an online credit reference account, you need to check if you are on the Electoral Roll. [43] You can now do this online or contact your local council. Ensure that if you move address, you re-register and check your details are still registered every year. <u>The credit reference agencies will give you more points on your score the longer you have been at the same address and registered on the Electoral Roll.</u>

---

[43] https://www.gov.uk/register-to-vote

Turbo-charge Your Credit, Step 3:

Check your financial associations.

If you have joint credit accounts with someone, they will appear on your financial associations list. If they have bad credit, it may prevent you getting finance. Just living with someone shouldn't put them on this list. Check that any financial associations listed are accurate. If they are not, you should remove them.

Turbo-charge Your Credit, Step 4:

Check your public records.

If you have had a CCJ, Bankruptcy, or IVA[44], this may appear on your file for up to <u>six years</u> and affect your credit score. We saw earlier in this chapter how to repair or even remove CCJ's. Ensure your public records are accurate. If you cannot change or remove them as described, your only option is to wait until the six years has expired and they will drop off your credit file automatically. If they do not drop off, contact the credit reference agency who will remove them for you.

---

[44] Individual Voluntary Arrangement

Turbo-charge Your Credit, Step 5:

Check all your credit accounts.

It is important to realise that various factors as to how you run your credit accounts will affect your credit score. If you have chosen a decent online account to check your file, you will be able to keep track of these main factors and more.

The length of time you have had a credit account. New applications will decrease your credit score - old accounts will increase your credit score. Do not cancel old accounts unless absolutely necessary! If you have no credit accounts or limited history you need to get some as described earlier.

The number of credit accounts you are using. If you have a number of credit accounts that are showing a balance above zero, this will decrease your credit score. Aim to pay it off and if possible, do not close the account. For example, you could pay off a credit card and keep the account active with a balance of zero; this should increase your score within a month or two. Having a high number of accounts with a zero balance will not affect your score negatively. *Even accounts with a low balance such as £1 can impact your score negatively, I've also seen negative balances affect credit files (i.e. a positive balance and in credit), so* ensure you pay them off exactly to zero.

The proportion of the credit you are using. Your score will be decreased if you are using a high proportion of your available credit. Try to keep your credit balance below 50% and if at all possible, below 30% of your available limit. Doing this will increase your credit score quickly. 'Maxing out' your credit will impact your credit heavily (maybe 30-40 points), so only do it if you really have to, and get it back down as soon as possible afterwards.

Late payments. Ensure that you pay everything on time.
If you time your payments carefully, and depending on when the lender reports to the CRA's, you can show a lower balance if you pay before the <u>due date</u> on your statement. Be careful not to pay before your <u>statement</u> date, or this will go towards the previous month's statement. Keep credit applications to a minimum. Always apply with providers that do a search that will not impact your credit file first (soft

search). Only apply if your score indicates that you have a good chance of success. Often, two applications on the same day will not impact you as much as two applications spread out by a couple of weeks or months. Time your applications wisely. If you do apply, the searches will dent your credit file for six months. Therefore, once you have applied, do not apply again for at least six months. Ensure searches that appear on your file are legitimate, if not, contact the CRA to have them removed.

Debts at Previous Addresses and Fraud.

You should check you have no debts at previous addresses. Previous addresses are linked to your current address, so check these are accurate and query any mystery addresses. You should also check that you have not been a victim of identity fraud and whether you appear on the fraud register CIFAS.[45] Appearing on the database should not decrease your credit score. However, the lender will carry out more checks to ensure the application is genuine. Contact CIFAS or the lender who registered you to be removed from the register.

Turbo-charge Your Credit, Step 6: **Don't Forget.

Your Limited Company Credit File.

You also need to ensure you check your limited company credit file. Similar principles apply, so you can apply the techniques used above to your business credit file too. You will need to register for a separate online credit file service for your business. Unlike the consumer market, the business market mainly offers paid options. I have found that Experian offers a good service called My Business Profile.

---

[45] https://www.cifas.org.uk/nfd

My Business Profile.[46]

Pros: - An online account for limited companies that you can check as much as you like. You also get the advantage of alerts should anything change on your business file. One-off reports are also an option. You can cancel at any time.

Cons: - It's not cheap. Costs around £30 per month + VAT for thirty days service.

You have to decide if this is for you. If you are looking to apply for funding from banks and other lenders, you can be sure they will be checking <u>both</u> your personal file and company credit file, so it's probably wise to get your house in order sooner rather than later. Also, bear in mind that some business loans may appear on your personal file, rather than on your company credit file. We saw earlier that certain finance products from certain providers appeared on your business credit file. Always double check before accepting where the funding will be reported. It is probably better that you keep your personal and business finances separate, however, this is not always possible depending on the lender and their lending policies. Some just prefer to lend to an individual for businesses purposes rather than limited companies.

Just ensure that you are aware that a business loan on your personal file, for example, may rule you out from any personal finance you may need in future. Funding on your business credit file does not affect your liability since lenders will always insist on a guarantee from you as a director via a signed declaration, that you will pay personally should the company go bust. It just means that your personal credit file is free from the ebb and flow of business credit activity.

---

[46]https://www.mybusinessprofile.com/

Conclusion:

If you follow everything above, most people should be able to increase their credit score within 30-60 days. Remember to keep an eye on your file. If you are running a limited company, you would also be advised to check the file for your limited company regularly and apply the main points above to increase your company's score accordingly. Ensure you understand the risks associated with taking on funding, and you are aware as to which credit file the funding will be reported to (business or personal credit file).

> Remember, customers, suppliers, estate agents, and employers check credit files these days, so a good score can really help to move you forward in life as well as in business.

Spend, Spend, Spend

So, you now have the idea that's going to set you free. You have the funds to start. What would you spend them on? A flashy website? A new laptop? Business software? Swanky premises? New office furniture? A nice business suit?

I think you know the answer – none of the above!

As a rule, generally when starting up, minimise all spending on things your customers or clients don't see. So, if you have a web business, do not buy the latest all-singing, all-dancing laptop, or the latest accounts software for thousands of pounds. But do spend money on a good functional website that your customers will see. Not a flashy one.

Remember, a functional website is not one that looks pretty; it's one that generates cash! That doesn't mean you should create ugly websites, but ensure your website is geared towards sales, rather than pictures and dancing animations. Ensure you make it as easy as possible for your customer to buy from you.

> At the start, money is tight so don't try to be perfect. The trick is to create a veneer of professionalism for little or no cost. Remember, your start-up capital was hard to come by. Don't blow it all at once!

Buy, Beg, Or Steal

Tips on purchasing:

1) Do not buy the latest computer, unless your business demands it.

2) Try free and trial software before you invest or splash out.

3) Ask for a discount on everything. If you don't ask, you don't get! For some reason in the UK, we are very shy about doing this. I make a habit of asking for a discount on every purchase. You do get one most of the time, especially on large or cash purchases.

Tip: It is often harder to get a discount at large superstores, so go to smaller shops and get talking to the owner or sales reps who will often bite your hand off to get a sale!

4) Buy second-hand: This is a big one. There is absolutely no need to buy most things new. Search auction sites like eBay and save a fortune on your start-up costs.

5) Use the internet and comparison websites for the best price research. Use this price to haggle even more off!

6) VAT: Register for VAT and you can claim 20% off everything you buy for your business. The downside is you will have to charge your customers VAT and do extra paperwork and file returns to Her Majesty's Revenue and Customs (HMRC).

7) Pound shops: if you utilise these, you can save a fortune on consumables, such as batteries, blank CDs, padlocks, light bulbs etc.

Things you should NOT spend a fortune on when starting:

- Computers
- Software
- Office furniture
- Premises
- Staff
- Stock
- Tills and other systems

Spend huge amounts of money on these, and you could find that if there is no business coming in, you will be short of cash very quickly!

If you have borrowed to purchase these items at huge cost, the problem is compounded and you could be out of business even sooner.

Problem Solving:

Buying goods for your business comes with certain risks, so it is often a good idea to understand your rights when you are purchasing from suppliers. Also, it is important to note that your rights as a consumer may be different to those as a business.

The main legislation for the selling of goods on a business to business basis is the Sale of Goods Act.[47]

This act was replaced <u>for consumers only</u> by the Consumer Rights Act in 2015. This means that consumers have different rights when buying goods than businesses.

For Business to Business Selling:

The seller of the goods must meet the following:

---

[47] Sale of Goods Act 1979

Right to sell – The seller must have the right to sell the goods and must be the owner of the goods (hold legal title)[48]

The goods must match the description-[49]

The goods must be of satisfactory quality-[50] *(only applies if the seller is a business).*

-Fit for the purpose the goods are normally supplied.
-The appearance and finish must be satisfactory.
-Must be free from minor defects.
-Must be safe.
-The goods must be durable.

If you buy by sample, the goods must match the sample -[51]

Where goods are defective or not satisfactory, you the buyer will have no claim if the defects have been pointed out by the buyer, and/or you have examined the goods prior to purchase.

Otherwise, you, the business buyer, can reject the goods with a refund, and/or claim damages, or claim damages and repair of the goods.

S15a states that you cannot reject goods where the defect is so slight as to be unreasonable. [52](A consumer can reject goods within the first 30 days of supply).[53]

---

[48] s12 Sale of Goods Act 1979
[49] ibid s13
[50] ibid s14 (2B)
[51] ibid s15
[52] s15a Sale of Goods Act 1979
[53] Chapter 2 s22 Consumer Rights Act 2015

The Supply of Goods and Services Act[54] states that suppliers must carry out the service with "reasonable care and skill".

Digital content is covered by the Consumer Rights Act 2015 – However, surprisingly at present, there appears to be no protection **for businesses.**[55]

Conclusion

Where you buy from a private seller, your rights regarding quality and fitness for purpose may be diminished. If you buy goods knowingly that are defective, you may not be able to claim a refund or reject the goods. When you buy services, the services must be carried out with reasonable care and skill. It is important to remember that when you buy as a business, you may have fewer rights than when you buy personally as a consumer, so be careful and discuss with your legal advisor to avoid costly mistakes.

---

[54] s13 Supply of Good and Services Act 1982
[55] Chapter 3 -Consumer Rights Act 2015

WHAT TO SPEND ON?

We Can Work It Out

In the early days of a start-up, it is easy to get carried away with the start-up process; setting up the office, the new computer, the software, and accounts systems etc. It all looks great and then realisation hits: it's of no use if there are no customers.

So, the simple answer is you spend money on what makes you money, and that's it! This means that in your early days, the best way is to test the market before you splash out big time – simples!

But how do you do it in a practical sense? Well, you need a marketing strategy, but at this stage you have no idea what will work and what won't, so you TEST; there is nothing like real data from your own business:

First, decide the best way you could promote your business. Examples include:

1) Magazine advertising.
2) Internet advertising.
3) Flyers.
4) Email marketing.
5) Cold-calling.

Pick out a strategy that you think suits your business and just try it on a small scale and measure the results. For example:

You test-promote your business by printing 500 flyers costing £60. You distribute all 500 flyers and get ten enquiries and four sales at £30 each, therefore:

Number of flyers: 500
Cost of campaign: £60
Sales of campaign: £120
Number of enquiries: 10
Cost per lead: £6

This is information gold. Yes, you haven't made a fortune, but you know this campaign has some potential, especially if you can repeat this on future campaigns.

After this example test you can deduce:

If you print and distribute 5,000 flyers at £600 cost, you should generate 100 enquiries and make sales of £1,200 !

Remember, if you ask for a discount when ordering your bulk order of flyers, you can increase your profit!

This is just an example, but the principle is the same for all strategies. Test first in the real world and when you know what works, go for it.

If a particular strategy does not work, change your design or pitch and try again. If it still does not work, try another strategy until you hit one that does work.

Remember, marketing strategies are not always obvious. The ones listed are only examples and there are many more. Competitors are not eager to tell you how they get their business! So test, test, test, until you find a winning formula, and then farm it out, big time!

Try not to rely on one strategy, but try to develop several; just in case one strategy goes dry or gets too competitive. In this testing phase of your business, you should be 100% focused on results and the appearance of your business to the customer. All other money spent is probably wasted. If you find a winning strategy in this way, your business will become much more predictable and you will be able to grow in a logical way. Without this method, your business will be haphazard and unpredictable. Sorry, but it's true!

Remember, do not expect huge results from your test marketing. Responses of between 1–10% are normal.

Obviously, if you get no results from a number of strategies, it's time to rethink your business model!

Problem Solving:

Marketing Strategies. When carrying out our marketing strategy, it is important that we stay within the law and we don't break any rules, otherwise, our marketing plans could come crashing down. The relevant legislation is the Communications Act 2003. The rules for advertising are listed in The CAP (Committee of Advertising Practice) Code[56] for non-broadcast (print, email text, etc.). The code states that:

Marketing materials should be honest and truthful.

Marketing materials must respect the spirit of the code.

No marketing materials should bring advertising into disrepute.

There are specific rules regarding certain industries, so if your business involves marketing to children, involves food, gambling, alcohol, or finance, special attention should be given to these requirements. If you are planning marketing around TV and radio, this is covered by the BCAP (Broadcast Committee of Advertising Practice) code.[57]

Interestingly, both codes state that "obvious exaggerations" are <u>allowed</u> in your marketing, provided the consumer is unlikely to take the claim seriously, and the claims do not "materially mislead".[58]

With that in mind, let's take a look at the different types of marketing we can carry out and their pros and cons. The rise of the internet has given small businesses great opportunities to compete with the big boys, and in the three years it has taken to get this book finished, that advancement has only got bigger and better.

---

[56] https://www.cap.org.uk/Advertising-Codes/Non-Broadcast.aspx
[57] https://www.cap.org.uk/Advertising-Codes/Broadcast.aspx
[58] Committee of Advertising Practice Code 3.2
[59] https://www.google.co.uk/adwords/get-started

Digital Marketing – Is a term used to describe marketing on the internet, but could also include mobile phones, texts, etc.

AdWords.[59]

A product created by Google that allows you to place adverts in the search results. (I will cover more on AdWords later.)

Pros: - You only pay for the people who actually click on your ad. The advert can be targeted to geographical regions. A campaign can be set up with no upfront costs and clicks can cost only a few pence per click.

Cons: - Campaigns can be attacked by click fraud (where a competitor clicks on your ad repeatedly to diminish your budget). There is no detailed way to select the demographic of the consumer. If not managed correctly, large bills can be easily racked up.

Facebook/Instagram.[60]

Pros: - Facebook ads give a very targeted approach to marketing. You can specify age, location, gender, even interests. A campaign can be set up with minimal costs, from a few pence per click. You can place text or video ads.

Cons: - If not managed correctly, it can be easy to rack up huge costs. It is important to set appropriate budgets to begin with. You will need a Facebook business page to get going.

---

[60] https://www.facebook.com/business/products/ads

YouTube.[61]

Pros: - You can create video ads that can be targeted to consumers by interests, age, and location. The consumer can get a better look at the product and how to use it. You can set your daily budget and pay per view.

Cons: - Creating video content can be time-consuming and costly.

Online classifieds Ads: Gumtree[62]**, Loot.com**[63]**, UK Classifieds.**[64]

Pros: - Can often be free for limited campaigns. Can be good for local advertising reach. You can post on multiple free sites to increase your reach for no cost whatsoever.

Cons: - Often not effective unless the paid for option is used. Much less targeted than social media ads.

Print Advertising.

Do not dismiss traditional print advertising. This can be successful depending on your business. Trade magazines, club magazines, local newspapers, etc.

Pros: - You can reach consumers in very specialist or niche markets. Can be effective if your consumers are likely to be non-internet based.

Cons: - Can be expensive. You pay regardless of effectiveness.

<u>**Direct Marketing**</u>- is a term used where the consumer is contacted directly.

---

[61] https://www.youtube.com/yt/advertise/en-GB
[62] https://www.gumtree.com/
[63] http://loot.com/
[64] https://www.ukclassifieds.co.uk

Email marketing.

Pros: - Relatively cheap to implement.

Cons: - Must comply with The Privacy and Electronic Communications (EC Directive) Regulations 2003. The consumer must have given permission to be contacted, or the email address collected during the course of a sale. All correspondence must contain identifying details, the name of the company, and address. Consumers must be able to opt out.

Cold-calling.

Pros: - Instant consumer feedback on the product or service.

Cons: - Can be time-consuming. There are numerous legal restrictions. A consumer cannot be contacted if they are on the Telephone Preference Service. Unsolicited calls are restricted by The Privacy and Electronic Communications (EC Directive) Regulations 2003.

Postal Mailing lists.

Pros: - Physical presence in the consumer's premises. Can be effective if used correctly, catalogues, price lists, brochures, etc. Households or businesses can be targeted by demographic, size, etc.

Cons: - There are legal restrictions. You cannot contact anyone who is on the Mail Preference Service. Can be expensive to buy the lists, the printing, and the postage. There is potential for the consumer to perceive your material as 'junk' mail.

Flyers/posters.

Pros: - Can be an effective way of getting your message out to the general public. There are numerous legitimate agencies that allow you to post on billboards and other on-street locations. (Primesight[64] and Signkick[65]. for example.)

Cons: - You cannot simply place adverts anywhere you wish without permission. The Town and Country Planning Act[66] make it illegal to do so.[67]

Networking with Business Cards. Using sites such as- Meetup.com.[68]

It surprises me how many businesses, including large ones, do not have business cards.

Pros: - Cheap, can be fun meeting new people.

Cons: - Time consuming, need to be focussed to get results.

Your own website.

Pros: - Can be relatively inexpensive to create a website these days. You have full control over the customer experience.

Cons: - It can be difficult to drive customers to your site.

If you store information, you must comply with the Data Protection Act,[69] and you may have to be registered.[70]

---

[64] http://www.primesight.co.uk/
[65] https://www.signkick.co.uk/
[66] s220 Town and Country Planning Act 1990
[67] S224(3) ibid
[68] https://www.meetup.com
[69] Data Protection Act 1998
[70] https://www.gov.uk/data-protection-register-notify-ico-personal-data

Your site should also contain a privacy policy with your company name and address details. Your website must also offer terms and conditions to the consumer and must comply with distance selling regulations. (A Consumer rights policy that allows the consumer to return goods purchased online.)[71] If you store credit card details, you must ensure your computer server utilises SSL encryption. If you use 'cookies', (software on your website that can be used to keep track of user data), users should be able to accept or decline their use.

Radio advertising/TV advertising.

Pros: - High credibility in the eyes of the consumer.

Cons: - Costs of production and advertising may be high. As discussed previously, must comply with the BCAP.

Conclusion

When testing out your marketing strategies, it is important that you do not inadvertently flout the various rules and regulations. Remember to always seek permission to contact anyone via email, phone, postal mail, etc. and give them the facility to opt out. If you get it wrong and there are complaints to the Information Commissioners Office, you could be fined up to £5000 for *each* unsolicited contact.[72]

---

[71] Consumer Contracts (Information, Cancellation and Additional Charges) Regulations 2013
[72] https://ico.org.uk/action-weve-taken/nuisance-calls-and-messages

Websites such as Fiverr[74] can help keep the development costs of your marketing materials down in the early stages of your company's development.

[74] https://www.fiverr.com/

Comic Book Page 6

The time machine activates...

Sends Unlimited Hero back in time...

Unlimited Hero uses a special sonic signature (Sound wave device) to hypnotise some help...

Unlimited Hero hypnotises 5 people, who each tell 5 people. Thousands appear..

Doctor Mort is surrounded by thousands...

Nooooo!

Unlimited Hero snatches the CCJ.

DOING THE MATHS

Human Equation

Do not get put off by the title – maths, ugh! This chapter is life-changing! Focusing on results is essential in the early days for survival. Often, having very little to start off with is a benefit, as it focuses the mind on questioning every penny spent.

As discussed previously, the result of your marketing strategy is gold. The reason is because of this equation:

Number of leads x conversion rate = number of humans buying!

It's so obvious, but this is life-changing! Do not skip this page, fall asleep, or yawn! This equation almost blew my mind when I discovered it at a business seminar. Bear with me one minute.

If you have tested your marketing strategy, you will know your conversion rate or will be able to work it out. In our previous example, we printed: 500 flyers at £60 = cost £60

Generated 4 sales = £120
Number of enquiries = 10

Our conversion rate is 4/500 flyers or 0.008

So, 500 flyers x 0.008 = 4 paid customers

Therefore, just say we wanted 20 customers a week, we would need:

No of flyers = 20/0.008 or 2,500 flyers

Therefore, 2,500 flyers would generate 20 paid customers a week at £30 each, or in this case = *£600 per week!*

What is important about this equation is that it empowers you to grow your business. You can increase your business by increasing the number of leads (flyers), or by increasing your conversion rate. At first, it will be easier to increase your leads, but as you tweak your marketing, you can increase your conversion rate by improving your copy, improving the design, or by targeting individuals who are more likely to buy.

Also, we can see from this equation:

Number of humans buying x number of transactions per customer x average cost of sale = turnover

So, in this case:

20 customers x 1 sale per customer x £30 per sale = £600 turnover

Therefore, if you can get each customer to buy from you twice:

20 customers x 2 sales x £30 = £1,200 turnover

But, what if you wanted a £1,000,000 business?

Number of customers x 2 sales per customer x £30 = 1,000,000

Customers = 1,000,000/(2 x 30) = 16,666 customers

But, how many flyers would that require?

16,666/0.008 = 208,325 flyers needed

You can see that by changing one or two variables of the equation, you can TURBO-CHARGE your business. However, you must know your conversion rate first. Don't go by chance or guess. So, in this example, by just testing with 500 flyers, we can predict that if we get 16,666 customers from 208,325 flyers, we can generate £1,000,000! I told you it was life-changing!

Now of course there could be problems with our assumptions. Maybe the cost of distributing 208,325 flyers is prohibitive, or the market may not be large enough or contain 16,666 customers, but in principle this works.

If you use this you will not be praying for business to come in. Your business will be much more predictable.

Problem Solving:

Sales Contracts.

It's one thing working out how to get the sales. But a common mistake many fledgling entrepreneurs make is failing to recognise the basics of contract law, understanding when they do or do not have a binding contract with a customer, and then how to enforce it should the customer decide not to pay.

Many people believe that if something is not in writing, then it is not a contract and cannot be enforced - <u>wrong!</u>

So, what forms a contract, then? Well, you need these five things. If you have all of these, then there is a valid contract whether or not you have a written agreement:[75]

<u>There must be some kind of offer.</u> – i.e. I <u>will</u> sell my shoes for £40.

<u>There must be acceptance of the offer.</u> – i.e. OK then, let's do it.

<u>There must be the intention to create a contract-</u> i.e. You're looking to buy shoes. I'm looking to sell shoes.

<u>There must be 'consideration'.</u> i.e. Something in exchange –(usually money), but not always.

<u>There must be clear terms</u> i.e. I will give you the shoes if you give me the money.

Things are complicated significantly by the fact that some offers are not offers at all, but are classed as 'Invitations to treat',[76] a kind of pre – offer communication, such as a shop display or someone who says 'I may sell to you'.

---

[75] Carlill v Carbolic Smoke Ball Company [1892] <u>EWCA Civ 1</u>
[76] Fisher v Bell [1961] 1 QB 394

So, you have to be careful as to what you agree to verbally, don't just think 'it's OK, there's nothing in writing'. Also, if someone has promised to deliver something for your business, you may have a contract and be entitled to damages should they not deliver. Ensure you draw up agreements for all of your business activities with clear terms. If you cannot do this for whatever reason, always send written confirmation of what you have agreed via email, so if there is any dispute you can refer to it later.

Getting paid.

Sometimes, despite having a clear agreement and having delivered the goods, a bad client will just refuse to pay. What happens then? Well, the first step is to communicate; send them:

<u>Written</u> communication of your agreed terms and a demand for the money.

Try and back it up with a reminder call and remember to stay calm during that call.

If there is no reply after fourteen days, send a final reminder and a warning of further action.

If there is still no reply, you have to decide if it is worth taking further action with this client. If you take action, you have to bear in mind your business relationship is likely to be 'toast'. You also need to differentiate those who can't pay from those who won't pay. There is no point chasing a payment when it is clear that they have no money to pay you, since it will cost you money to collect the money owed.

If you do decide to take things further, you can submit a claim through the 'Small Claims Court' also known as a money claim. You can submit your claim online[77] or via the paper form (Form N1). Ensure you provide full details of your case and the full details of the non-paying client. If the non-payer disputes your claim, there may be a hearing where you can put forward your case. If successful, judgment will be made in your favour and the defendant will be ordered to pay. If they do not, they will obtain a County Court Judgment (CCJ) against their name, which could prevent them from obtaining credit in the future.

Be aware that the fees vary depending on the amount of your claim and whether you apply online or in paper form. Fees range from £25 for an online claim of up to £300 to £10,000 for a paper claim of over £200,000. [78]

If you are going to go down this route, ensure you sue the correct person! Remember what we discussed earlier about separate legal identity (p50)? If your client is a limited company, make sure you sue the company and not the individual director or sales person. If you get it wrong, your case could be thrown out, since it is the company who owes you the money and not the individual.

Conclusion.

Try not to enter into verbal agreements as they could still be binding on you and your business. Draw up agreements for all your business dealings. Ensure you collect payment promptly from the client. Collecting payments is not for everyone, for some reason, there is real embarrassment about asking for money. To ease the pain, ensure you ask for the money (or part of it) upfront while you are signing or have agreed to the terms. Not only does this tick the box of our 'five wants' for a valid contract and indicates intention, but it also helps your stretched cashflow.

---

77 https://www.moneyclaim.gov.uk/web/mcol/welcome
78 https://www.gov.uk/make-court-claim-for-money/court-fees

Remember, going to court should be the last resort, you need to try and resolve the problem with the client first and give written warning of any intended action. Also, bear in mind that civil cases are heard on the basis of 'balance of probabilities'; this means that if you can prove 51% that your claim is valid, you will win. However, the non-paying client has the same odds, so ensure your evidence is 'watertight', or the decision could go against you on a slight technicality.

ORGANISING YOURSELF

Organised Confusion

When I originally started my music business, I had no idea or strategy; I just started and hoped for the best. That's great, especially if you are passionate, but, if we want to make real money, we need to organise ourselves.

Keep an A4 notebook and write down all your tasks and all your goals and tick them off as you achieve them.

As you fill up each notebook, start a new one and number them. This is very important; when I started, I would jot ideas down on bits of paper and eventually would end up with loads of paper all over the place. I had no way of referring back to ideas or previous goals!

I would often revisit and go over the same ideas without even realising. It suddenly dawned on me that if I kept all my 'to do' lists and goals in one place (in a notepad), not only could I remember them, but I could also see at a glance how many of my goals I was achieving.

Writing everything in a book like this focuses your mind on the task at hand and you literally cannot wait to start ticking things off. Just make sure your goals are small steps rather than giant leaps, but do include everything, no matter how ridiculous, as it may develop into something.

I also staple any price quotes, web information, and research information into the notepad, so I have a complete record if I want to retrace my thought process. I also periodically refresh my list, adding new tasks, deleting completed ones and highlighting outstanding ones. At the start of the year, I have a 'to do' list and goal list for the entire year. Yes, things may crop up to delay or postpone your plans, but it is amazing how that once written down, your mind focuses on achieving the goal.

When starting out, your notebook may look like this:

1) Register limited company. (OK, done)

2) Research quotes for website. (OK, done)

3) Print business cards.

4) Print letterheads.

5) Find 50 clients for first year.

6) Print 500 flyers.

7) Test the market.

You will 'OK' and tick off your list as you complete the tasks, giving you a nice visual indication of your progress.

As your business grows, you will think of more and more tasks to grow your business. Also, your business itself will generate new tasks, so it is important to keep on top of things by writing it all down. It will come in handy when you are trying to remember how you completed a task, or trying to find that amazing company you came across on the web last year, but can't remember their name. Just look in your notebook.

YOUR DATABASE

Inspiration Information

Is there gold in them thar hills? Are the streets paved with gold? No, but there is gold in your database!

Database is just a fancy word for your client list. Don't think you have to spend a fortune on database software. A simple spreadsheet is fine initially for your start-up from zero. These days, for me, the most important aspect of your database is your email list. This is probably more important than your client's name and even their phone number – why?

Because emailing your clients is free, and as we know already:

Number of leads x conversion rate = PAID CUSTOMERS

So, if we have 5,000 email addresses and we email them with our offer and our conversion rate is 0.008 we will get:

5,000 x 0.008 = 40 paid customers

If we are offering a product or service at £50, that's £2,000 from almost zero marketing outlay.

There IS gold in your database!

The trick to building a database is to start one as soon as you start trading and not a day later! Note down:

- Every lead
- Every enquiry
- Every visitor
- Every paid customer

You should make it your priority to get their email addresses and add them to your database. Once you get into the habit, it's easy and only takes a second. If you have a website, you can include a form to collect visitor emails.

Remember, not all enquiries turn into sales right away. If you do not get your potential client's email address, you could literally be leaving gold or money on the table!

It's free, so ask and you shall receive. If your enquiry or potential client refuses, don't be pushy. Most people are happy to provide contact details as long as they are interested in your service.

> It never ceases to amaze me how many companies never ask for an email address. Turbo-charge yours and start collecting from day one.

Comic Book Page 7

His powers revived Julian Zero enables his eighties watch and transforms.

Hero sets out to find Doctor Mort and creates five Nano bots that replicate and sets them out to find and infect Dr Mort's computer systems.

106

MARKETING

To Catch A Virus

A friend of mine, who was running a new business, asked me what she should do, as she didn't have a marketing budget and wanted to promote her business to as many people as possible.

I said she should talk about her business more. Even as a friend of many years, I had no idea what she was doing business-wise and the services she offered. She should tell everyone she meets about her business venture. I don't think it registered, as the next time I spoke to her, she was contemplating spending hard-earned cash on advertising.

Now, don't get me wrong. Advertising can and does work. But it costs, and mistakes, when you are starting from zero, hurt –trust me, I've been there. Let's look at it this way, suppose I have a new business and tell five people about my business, but ask these five people to tell just five of their friends. How many people will know about my business if this is done five times?

Me
Five friends
Each of these five friends tells five people = 25 people
Each of these 25 people tells five friends = 125 people
Each of these 125 people tells five friends…etc. etc.

Well, you end up with 3,905 people!

We know from the previous chapter that our conversion rate is 0.008 and if they all get to hear about our offer that's:

3,905 leads x 0.008 = 31.25 new customers

If our offer is priced at, say, £40 per customer, that's £1,249.60! *From word of mouth alone!*

It definitely is good to talk!

The beauty of this is that you don't even need to know a lot of people: three to five friends is fine. Just get them to tell people they know and it never costs you a penny!

I used this system to great effect when doing events. I booked five bands and got them to tell friends and their fan base. The above effect would kick in, attracting great attendance at the door.

Of course, the system is flawed. If one round of people does not tell the next round, or your message is not interesting enough, the campaign will stop dead in its tracks.

> If you have very interesting content, your service could go 'viral' and attract huge attention.

Email From Heaven

Many schools of thought dismiss emails, but in my experience, email is the one web tool that works and is great to do business with.

People tend to take email seriously. Facebook, Twitter feeds, and other forms of social media are often ignored or treated lightly. So, if you send a good email, the chances are you will get some kind of response. *These techniques can also be implemented for the other forms of marketing mentioned previously.*

Formatting your message:

1) Make your message important!

You can do this by clicking the '!' before you send your message. Your message will appear with a red exclamation mark in your recipient's inbox and make your message stand out from the crowd!

2) Ensure your subject contains your company name and something relevant to the recipient.

Even if your recipient is not interested in your service and never opens your email, having your company name in the subject will raise the awareness of your company and they may open your message next time. Place a simple line after your company name to entice your recipient.

Example: 'XYZ Ltd Amazing Deal Just For You'

3) Always remember to add a call to action in your email.

If you don't spell it out, most people will do nothing. So, if you want your recipient to go to your website, ensure you place a link to the exact page they need to go to and tell them what to do.

Example: 'Click on the link below now for our special offer.'

Ensure you time-limit the offer so they don't put it off and invariably forget!

Example: 'Apply within two hours of this email and get a further 5% off.'

4) Try and make the email personal.

Include their first name (Dear John), rather than first and last name (Dear John Smith) or just 'Dear customer'. If the email is personal it is more likely to be read. If you can include some additional information about them, such as previous items purchased, even better.

Example 'Dear John, thanks for your recent purchase of ZYZ product, I am contacting you because…'

You can get mail merge software to automate the process for you without having to create loads of personalised emails by hand. Just ensure you have set it up correctly so you have correct names and information in the right places, and no funny characters and spaces, as this will ruin your email campaign.

5) Don't spam.

Just because most people take email seriously, do not be tempted to spam or send unsolicited emails to all and sundry. Not only will they potentially get angry; if you upset too many people, your internet service provider (ISP) may cut you off!

Always ensure your email lists contain those who genuinely want to be contacted and delete promptly those who do not.

If your marketing involves sending thousands of bulk emails, consider setting up your own mail server and IP address or enlist a bulk email provider, to avoid problems with your ISP. Many ISPs restrict sending emails in bulk and may block you, even if your list is not spam!

Problem Solving:

Remember to stay within the law. As discussed previously, marketing communications, including email, are covered by the
The Privacy and Electronic Communications (EC Directive) Regulations 2003. You need to get permission to send the message, or the email must have been collected in the course of a business transaction. You need to give the customer the ability to opt-out.

Concepts such as 'call to action' or time limited 'special offers', apply to other marketing methods, not just email, so remember to use them in other forms of advertising. Collect your customer's email address from the beginning, keep the list updated, and don't be tempted to bombard your customer unnecessarily.

Running out of cash. When sales are not enough.

Sometimes, despite all of our testing and marketing efforts, sales are not forthcoming, and our start-up funds begin to diminish. If this is happening to you, the first thing to do is:

DO NOT BURY YOUR HEAD IN THE SAND AND CONTINUE TO DO THE SAME THING!

Sorry for all of the caps, but this is your hard to come by capital at stake here. We need to change something to get out of the rut. The sooner you can get to grips with this the better. Do not leave any changes to the last minute; it could be too late. Above all, stay calm and rational, it's easy to panic when things are not going to plan. Go through the following steps to grind out the problems:

Step 1:

Revisit your customer database. If you have made sales, but just not in significant quantities, try to gain data from your customers about your product or service. Why did they buy?
How do they rate the product? Are they using the product in the way you envisaged?

Don't forget to get data from those that did not buy. Why did they not buy from you? Was it the price? Was some element missing from the product? What would make them buy? You need this information to work out whether there is an inherent fault with your product, or is it the way the customer perceives your product, or is it just a marketing problem where the customer is not connecting with your marketing.

If you have made no sales at all, it is important you get data from those that didn't buy and 'listen' with a dispassionate ear. Sometimes, it can be hard hearing criticism, but if things are not going right, we have to listen. It is important you do not try to guess why there are no sales since you could waste valuable time and resources working out what the problem is, rather than just a couple of calls to clients who more often than not will tell you right away what the problem is.

Step 2:

Adjust your marketing materials in line with the feedback you have received from your clients or non-clients. At this point, it's probably not a good idea to tinker with the product yet, since it could be that the solution is just a matter of getting the marketing copy and pricing right. Do not make the mistake of thinking that the cheapest is best; all customers want the very best price. You have to work out what unique elements your product offers that justifies the highest price possible. You then have to convey those unique elements to the customer, so she understands the value of your proposition. If your feedback really does indicate that the price is too high, do not drop the price right away, offer a time limited deal and test if that makes a difference in sales.

Step 3:

If you have a number of items of feedback from your customers, try to implement them one by one, so you can ascertain what works the best. Some forms of marketing work better for some industries than others, so try altering your marketing mix to test if that makes a difference. Go back to Step 2 and test again.

Step 4:

If you still have no sales, you will have to take a good hard look at the product. If possible, adjust your product in-line with the feedback given by customers. Revisit Step 2 and include any new features in your marketing copy.

Step 5:

If after these four steps there is still no traction, maybe the customers you are targeting simply have no immediate need for your product. If that is the case, try to imagine a customer you are not targeting that could use your product. Sometimes, just changing the 'type' of person you contact could make all the difference. For instance, if you have developed a shampoo for trade and it is not selling, maybe it would sell better as a 'professional' shampoo for consumers. Maybe you need to provide another service or product alongside your offering to make it more compelling to the customer, such as a bundle. Or maybe your service or product can be used in a completely different way than you envisaged given a few tweaks. Maybe, in this evaluation process, you discovered all your potential clients are crying out for a particular type of product but not yours. Now is the time to listen to that feedback and implement it.

Conclusion.

If after all this evaluation there are still no sales, do not be afraid to scrap the idea and try something else. Since you have not overspent on equipment or marketing, and since you are just in the testing phase, this is annoying, but it should not be fatal. At least you know there is just no market for this offering.

YOUR TIME

Wiser For The time

Your time is your most precious commodity. Once expended, you cannot get it back. So, from the outset, ration your time wisely.

I came across a theory that states 15% of what we do is productive, while 85% of what we do is not so productive. Try and prioritise your work so you concentrate on the 15%. (Your A4 notebook mentioned earlier is useful for this.)

I have also seen this theory described as the 80–20 rule. Italian economist Vilfredo Pareto[79] discovered the concept way back in 1896 when he realised that 80% of Italian land was owned by 20% of the population. 80% of your business will come from 20% of your customers. The key to saving your time and effort is to concentrate on the 15–20% most important tasks and customers and multiply them.

Try to prioritise your time and have a set schedule for meetings. Do not let people eat up your time. If you have a scheduled 30-minute meeting, have a half-an-hour meeting; anything more than that is time wasted.

Also, is there any point in having a meeting with a client for one hour if he is only going to spend £20 with you? Sometimes, in our eagerness to attract business, we will do almost anything to get a sale. However, time is the one thing we cannot get back. We can get back possessions, money if lost, but time we cannot, and it's limited; so think before you spend your time, your precious commodity, with anyone.

It also helps to break down your time on a cost per hour basis, even if you are not paid by the hour. For example, a client phones in and says he's interested in your business proposal, but wants to meet you first. Your proposal is for £100, the client arrives one hour late, and you talk for one hour. You have devoted two hours of your time to the client.

---

[79] Vilfredo Pareto, Cours d'économie politique *(1896–97)*

If your hourly rate is £20 p/h, your client has eaten up £40 of your time. That's nearly 50% of your £100 fee!

If your client books, you have made £60 instead of £100.

Worse still, if he goes away unconvinced, you have lost £40 of your time that you can never get back!

High Priority

The trick to prioritising your time is:

1) NO impromptu meetings.

2) Keep all meetings on time and on schedule.

3) Stack your tasks and meetings so you do those in the same location, or in a similar vein on the same day.

4) Do not let late arrivals impact on your own diary. Close the meeting at the agreed time.

5) Choose and carry out regular tasks at a set time and schedule as daily, weekly, or monthly.

6) Be on time yourself.

7) Use your A4 notebook and keep a 'to do' list of important tasks.

8) Prioritise all tasks and do all those that will generate cash and those that relate to customer experience first.

While we are on the subject of time, when working for yourself it's easy to get into 'job mode'. By that I mean thinking the more hours you put into the business, the more money you will make. We have already seen that if you have structured your business to set you 'free', that is simply not the case. In fact, if structured correctly, your business should make you money while you sleep! We also saw that:

Number of leads x conversion rate = new customers

Nothing to do with your hours worked.

If we succumb to 'job mode', we end up working longer and longer hours, and 80% of our time will be non-productive and 20% will be productive. Obviously, running your own business is hard work and you will need to put plenty of hours in, but ensure you think about how you utilise your time.

Relax, Don't Do It

You should take at least one day off a week that you spend away from your business, with family, with friends or a partner. Do not look at emails, do not take business calls. Unless it is an absolute emergency!

A recent UK study showed that over 500,000 small business owners do not make social plans because they feel they are too busy, and a quarter of business owners surveyed said they fell ill due to work demands or stress.[80] Another UK report by Xero indicates that 58% of successful entrepreneurs state that time spent with family is a contributory factor to their success.[81]

Yes, I know it's hard to do, but trust me, it makes sense. The last thing you want is to end up working seven days a week, and on the umpteenth week without even a day off, a client phones you first thing on a Sunday morning, and when you don't answer, goes crazy as you were not available! It's happened to me.

From the outset, structure your business with time off, so all your customers are aware you are closed on the days you specify. Whatever days you decide, it is important to remember you will not lose business. In fact, most people will respect you for taking time off and spending it with your family and will happily call back on a Monday.

If you do not structure in time off, you will be run ragged and burn out very quickly and probably lose touch with your family and friends if you continue for long periods of time.

Remember, as we said earlier, time is your most precious commodity. Remember to save some for your family and friends and most importantly, yourself. You cannot buy time back when your business has 'made it'. It's too late – it's gone!

---

[80] http://www.simplybusiness.co.uk/about-us/press-releases/750,000-small-business-owners-missing-out-on-summer-holidays-with-children/
[81] https://www.xero.com/content/dam/xero/pdf/Xero-Make-or-break-report.pdf

Another advantage of taking time off is perspective and ideas. It's amazing how when relaxing in the bath, or when I wake up from a good sleep on a day off, an idea will pop into my head. Just jot it down in your notebook or make a mental note of it and deal with it when you get back to business.

Doing this means you will be itching to get back to business on Monday morning to follow up on that new idea. (How many people can say that?)

> You will need this positive energy to make things happen. Nurture it by taking adequate time off.

POSITIVE THINKING

Comic Book Page 8

The bots find Dr Mort's lair and computer systems through the drains and gutters. The bots get into his computers...

..And alert Hero who makes his way to Dr Mort's secret lair.

Intruders, I'll show them!

Mort injects negative energy into the room.

How do you fancy some of this mind drug Hero?

Agghhh!

POSITIVE THINKING

Good Vibrations

I am a strong believer in positive thinking. Staying positive is one of the most difficult things to achieve when everything is going wrong, but it is important to remain positive despite setbacks. Psychology academics such as Barbara L Fredrikson argue that positive thinking provides an 'upward spiral' of contentment whereby positive thinking contributes to seeking out new possibilities, which leads to more positive experiences, which in turn leads to seeking out more opportunities and more contentment.[82]

In short, positive thinking can expand our awareness and enable us to see the 'bigger' picture, essential requirements for running a business. So, although 'positive thinking' is an often used 'fluffy' term, it is highly important in my opinion. Try not to confuse positive thinking with blind optimism! It is still essential to 'keep it real' regarding your circumstances, just don't get too bogged down in the negative if things don't go your way occasionally; try and see a positive aspect to the situation.

Often negative thoughts will come into our lives:
'I can't do this.'
'I am going to fail.'
'I'm too old.'
'I'm too young.'

Or people will tell you:
'It's not good enough.'
'You're too old.'
'You're too young.'
'You will fail.'

---

[82] http://www.unc.edu/peplab/publications/Fredrickson%20AESP%202013%20Chapter.pdf

But you must banish the negativity and program your brain to think differently:

I will be good enough.
I've got maturity and experience.
I've got youth and enthusiasm.
I will succeed.

I strongly believe that a large part of what we achieve is down to our own thinking. I remember once I was handing out flyers in the street, I'd had a bad day and I tried like mad to hand out these flyers but hardly anyone would take them. This made me even more frustrated, which meant even fewer people took them!

You are not being naïve thinking positively. It is not just wishful thinking. You are programming your brain to see a positive solution rather than just a negative one. For instance:

You are trying to get a large order from a client. After much deliberation and back and forth, the order does not come through. You could deal with it in two ways:

1) Negative thinking: Give up and go to the next customer.

2) Positive thinking: Thank the client for considering you and offer a smaller package at a reasonable rate.

Remember: Business is about solving problems. People are happy to pay you money if you can solve their problems! So, think of positive solutions to setbacks.

There is a 'positive' to every 'negative', for example:

You fail a test or a task.

1) Negative: You are set back and are simply not good enough.
2) Positive: You will use the opportunity to get better. You will get good enough and use the experience to look at where you went wrong until you succeed!

Achieving something is just a series of small steps; often the reason we 'fail' is because we try and take too much of a leap.

Break everything down into small steps. Remember your 'to do' list? You are less likely to 'fail' using small steps.

See failures as setbacks that can be overcome with solutions or ideas. Do not try to be right all of the time. If you do fail, look at what you did wrong and analyse what you would do to improve it. Try to avoid blaming others for your failure – you will not learn and will be trapped in a cycle of failure, as we are not in control of others, only ourselves. In the example where I was handing out the flyers, it would be easy to blame the passers-by: 'Stupid people, take my flyers, I have a great offer!' Instead, look at yourself and change your outlook, then people will be happy to take from you!

Do you follow sport? For example, football, I find it fascinating that in the pre/post-match talk, players will often talk about 'mental strength' to defeat the opposition. They often talk about 'remaining positive'. This for me is an important key to success – why? Because, if you have two teams competing, both with multi-million-pound players of similar ability, the only difference between winning and losing is the mental strength, or the grey matter in between the ears!

WEIRD STUFF

Spirit In The Sky

OK, as promised at the start of the book, we are entering mystical territory here, or Woo Woo Land! It doesn't matter what religion you are, or if you don't believe in God at all. The most important thing in my mind is to 'ask for success'. This may sound weird and strange, but it works! It is important to allow yourself to want things and 'ask for them'; how you ask is up to you. In your head, out loud, shout, whisper, at night, first thing in the morning. These 'prayers' are important. Don't ask me how it works, I don't know. Some will say God, others say it's programming the brain or a self-fulfilling prophecy, or, even as discussed earlier, positive thinking; but it works. Often, we feel guilty for wanting things for fear of being labelled dreamers or unrealistic, but it is important to acknowledge your desires and ask for them.

I believe strongly:

You can achieve whatever you believe.

When you are stuck in business, just 'ask' for a solution and if you are 'listening' and are taking enough time off to distance yourself from the noise, often a solution will make itself apparent.

It's often frowned upon to want money or possessions, but there is nothing wrong in wanting these things. We need money and possessions to lead a healthy and comfortable life. By asking for something, we are setting a process in our mind and saying to ourselves that we definitely want it.

Admitting our dreams is often scary as we do not want to fail, shatter our dreams, look foolish, naïve, or to be denied. Asking opens the mind to the possibilities and your brain will do its best to bring those thoughts to reality.

You can ask for anything, just be specific. (Be careful for what you wish for!)

Wonders Of The Universe

There is a theory of quantum physics that says you cannot define the position of electrons in an atom. Electrons can be in many different places at once and at the same time. Since we are made of atoms and our atoms contain electrons, it means the positions of our electrons can be in several places at once!

The upshot of all this is the multiple universes theory. Austrian physicist Erwin Schrödinger, in his famous thought experiment 'Schrödinger's Cat', suggested that every event is a branch in the universe and that his imaginary cat was both alive and dead in different branches of the universe.[83] Technological advances such as quantum computers by companies such as D-Wave[84] also indicate the reality of multiverses.[85]

If this is true, there would be an infinite number of universes with slightly different versions of you: some rich, some poor, some working nine to five, some running your own business. If correct. it means every time we make a decision; the universe splits into all the different probabilities. So maybe asking for success splits us into the universe where we are successful because we made a conscious effort to accept it in our lives. I don't know, but from my experience, this works. Try it, and you'll see for yourself. This book is about my personal experience, and I've found this works for me. Try it, it's free; you have nothing to lose and everything to gain. Sometimes, opening up our minds to new theories and ways of thinking can lead to a different perspective on our problems.

These elements need to be in balance, before we can achieve 'true' success:

---

[83] http://hermes.ffn.ub.es/luisnavarro/nuevo_maletin/Schrodinger_1935_cat.pdf
[84] https://www.dwavesys.com/our-company/meet-d-wave
[85] https://www.youtube.com/watch?v=PqN_2jD

LIFE BALANCE

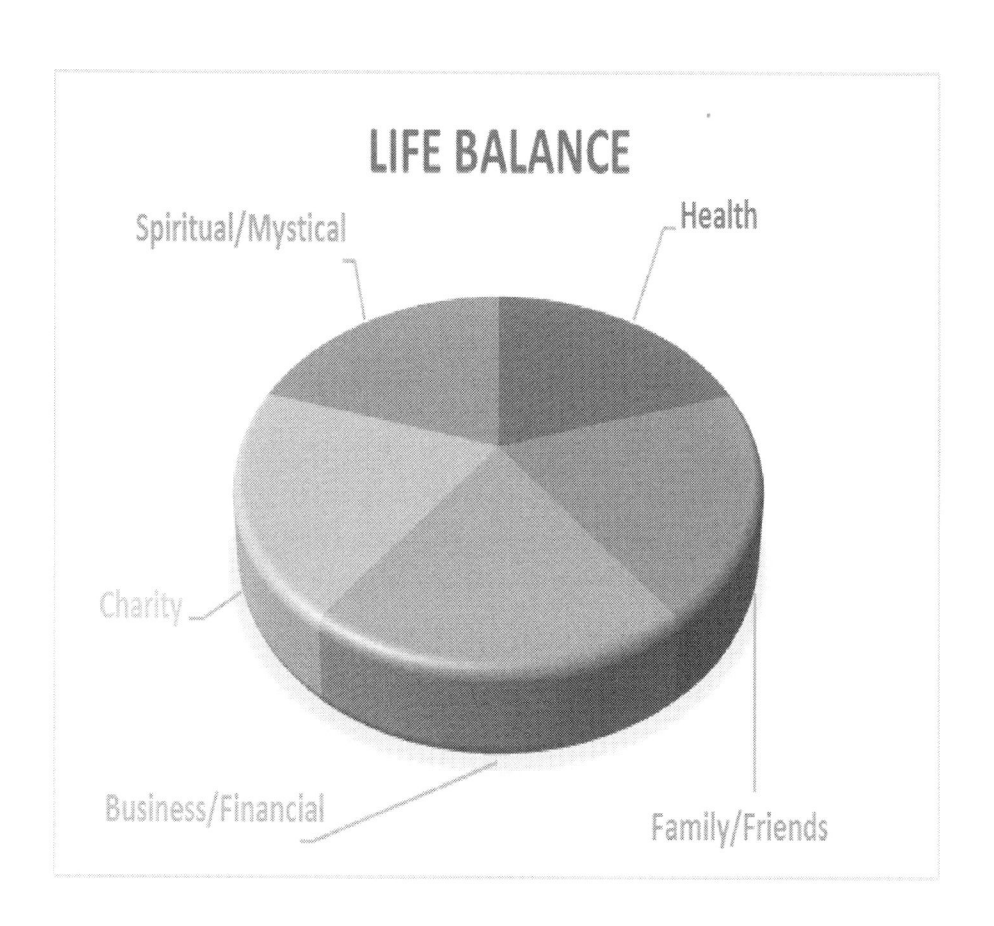

- Spiritual/Mystical
- Health
- Charity
- Business/Financial
- Family/Friends

HEALTH: PHYSICAL, AND MENTAL

In Sickness And In Health

It is easy whilst we are busy running around making money and growing our business to forget to look after ourselves. We discussed previously how important it is to take breaks so that we are rested. It is also very important that we nourish our physical and mental states, all of which will determine the outcome of our goals. It's no good having a great business if you are too sick or miserable to run it or grow it!

Problem Solving. My Story:

I am going to tell you a story, a true story. Let's rewind a few years back to Friday, May 8th, 2015; it was a reasonably warm sunny day for May. I had to complete a European Union Law exam that I was studying as a mature student at degree level. My new business project was doing well. I was deep in wranglings with Marvel and DC Entertainments Inc who were being stubborn regarding the title of this book; I was in a good relationship, all was seemingly good. Studying was hard, I was balancing the business with spending huge amounts of time reading intensely dense pieces of legislation.

I was also spending an increasingly large amount of my time on some particularly difficult clients. That Friday, after successfully completing the exam, I met up with friends for celebratory drinks, nothing too heavy, and had a great time. I got home before midnight and was looking forward to two weeks off from university study so that I could concentrate on me for a while. The weekend was nice, I went for a walk in the park with my partner and I was feeling relieved that a hard period of study was over for the time being.

On the morning of Monday 11th May, I woke up and for no apparent reason I had a strong feeling of dread. I just had this deep inner feeling that something very bad was going to happen. I spoke to my partner about it, and she reassured me that all was good at the moment and I continued with my day. The day ensued as normal; nothing bad happened, I was fine, everything was fine and normal. I had spent the day relaxing, watching movies, rubbish TV, etc. Later in the evening, I spoke to my brother on the phone, had dinner and a particularly nice piece of carrot cake, and fell asleep in my flat alone with the TV blaring out (bad habit).

At about five minutes past midnight, I woke up suddenly with the TV still blaring, went to the loo, and then went to pick up the remote control and BAM. I suddenly felt an intense pain in my chest. It felt like really bad indigestion. I thought to myself, "I shouldn't have had that last piece of carrot cake!" However, the pain would not go away; I could not lie down, I could not stay still. I raided the medicine cabinets for some Paracetamol, but it made no difference. I literally inched my way to the corner shop and breathlessly asked for some indigestion tablets. The shop assistant thrust the packet through the twenty-four-hour serving hatch, and I grabbed them and inched my way back.

On arriving home, I downed the pills with more painkillers and waited. There was a slight relenting, but I was still in agony. This did not seem normal, I tried to lie down again but it was too uncomfortable, I leant over to switch on the bedside lamp and BAM the bulb exploded, making the loudest bang I had ever heard from a perished light bulb. The exploding bulb must have tripped the circuit board, and I was suddenly plunged into complete darkness. I just sat there for thirty or so seconds, like an extra in some low budget horror movie, in agony, in complete darkness, waiting for I don't know what to come out of the pitch black. The feeling of dread had come back with a vengeance, and I felt totally and utterly defeated.

Then something kicked in, I fought back the pain, got some energy from somewhere and clambered through the darkness, feeling my way along the walls to the electricity cabinet downstairs, opened the door and flicked the trip switch, and to my relief, the lights came on again, Hallelujah! "I must go to the hospital, now." I thought to myself and made my way to the local cab station. No need for an ambulance, I was in agony, but fine. The ride was bumpy and painful, but fast. I entered Accident and Emergency, explained my symptoms to the receptionist and was asked to wait in reception. I squirmed painfully in my cold plastic seat while I waited to see someone for what seemed like an age.

Eventually, the doctor asked to see me, they took some blood tests, hooked me up to some machines and gave me some medication for the pain. About an hour later he returned, his demeanour was quiet and sad as he said, "Mr Jules, given your age and physical wellbeing, I am surprised, but I am afraid to say, you have suffered a heart attack." My head reeled, "Heart attack!" I thought to myself, no way, I did not feel as though I had a heart attack! Surprisingly, at that point, I did not panic, but felt incredibly calm; the real and genuine thought of facing death crossed my mind for probably the first time in my life, and I felt calm. I had tried to do everything I wanted to do in business. I had failed sometimes, but in other ways had succeeded. I had good friends and family, a wonderful partner, if today was going to be the day, so be it. I had had a good time with no regrets. My premonition, my feeling of dread, had manifested itself to be true. Something bad, something unimaginable had happened and it was going to be life changing.

The following months were hard; the heart attack had diminished my strength, I was on a cocktail of seven drugs a day, many of which I would have to take for the rest of my life, and I was in cardiac rehab with seventy to eighty- year olds. I just did not look like your typical heart attack victim; I wasn't overweight, I didn't smoke, and I ate reasonably healthily. However, I was seriously ill. I could not walk a hundred metres without feeling extremely tired and short of breath. I had to make a decision: was this it? Should I give up, on the business? On the Law Degree? On the case with Marvel and DC? Should I give up on everything I had worked for and succumb to this horrible illness?

Yes, the advice from family and friends and partner was; "You have to take it easy now", and I agreed, but the prospect made me feel utterly miserable. "I would rather die fighting for what I believe in than simply sitting passively in the wings while the rest of my life passes me by." I thought. Yes, I would have to be more careful, but I just had to continue. I just could not give up. In July I had to write an essay for the law degree coursework and the deadline was approaching, I gritted my teeth and although I had not been to a single lecture or tutorial, I researched the topic from home, taking frequent breaks. I was determined to succeed and finally submitted my essay. I must admit, I had experienced pain while writing, both physically and mentally, but in my mind it was worth it. It was something to aim for. Something to achieve when everything else seemed so hopeless.

I was surprised and dumbfounded to find out, when the results came out, that I had obtained one of the highest marks I had ever achieved and was awarded a distinction. I subsequently went on to pass my law degree, I won the trade mark Zero To Superhero® in the dispute with Marvel and DC Entertainments, I got rid of the difficult clients, and my business grew from strength to strength as I grew from strength to strength. I had to take better care of me but now I truly realised what it was really like to go from Business Zero To Superhero ®.

It is important to take some time to exercise. Physical activity will get the heart pumping. You will breathe in more oxygen which will flood the brain and help you think better, sharper, and will help you stay positive! Exercise can greatly affect your mood and performance so do it regularly to keep in reasonably good condition. We are not trying to win the Olympics! However, business is tough and you will need to have stamina and some physical strength to survive without burning out. So build some stamina by exercising.

Exercise will also flood your body with endorphins which will make you feel very good afterwards. Use this natural high to give you a lift at the start of your day. Looking and feeling good is important. In business, clients 'buy into' people so the better you look and feel, the better you will do.

You are your own billboard of your success!

Food For Thought

What we feed ourselves will also determine our mood. We have all heard of the phrase "we are what we eat"; what we put into our bodies will have an impact on our performance. Certain foods such as bread, pasta, and potatoes will make us sleepy whereas foods such as: fish, chicken, and bananas will give us energy and perk us up.

I'm not saying cut out 'sleepy food' but remember, if you are going to eat loads of pasta before tackling those boring accounts then don't be surprised if you fall asleep!

Likewise, if you are performing a physical task, you will probably need to 'bulk up' and eat more to get the energy to perform the task at hand.

Listen to your body and feed it accordingly, try not to go long periods without eating because you are too busy to eat. Ensure you always have breakfast so your metabolism can settle down and give you the energy and the best start to the day.

The Drugs Don't Work

These days, drugs are everywhere! Not just the illegal ones but the legal ones as well.

Legal: Cigarettes, alcohol
Illegal: Cannabis, cocaine

It is important to realise that taking drugs into the body will diminish its ability to function and affect your mood. At first, the effects will appear positive: Short-term confidence, short-term alertness. However, in the long-term the effects will always be negative. So avoid taking them altogether or at least minimise them to your days off.

If you are taking any illegal drugs you need to stop if you want to be successful and reach your goals. Drugs are not a class issue anymore; people of all classes and backgrounds take drugs. If you want to be in a better mental and physical state, they cannot be part of your plan.

I don't want to appear puritanical but this is a big issue for so many reasons:

- Financial: Drugs cost money, both legal and illegal. You can save a fortune by cutting them out. If you smoke 20 a day that's £5 x seven days = £35 a week, £140 a month, £1,680 a year! (Some start-up funding?)

- Relationships: People on drugs find it very difficult to build and maintain relationships; you are going to need to do just that to build your business.

- Health: The potential health implications of all drugs are well documented; drugs have the effect of making you feel better there and then but over time they will eat away at your physical and mental self.

Illegal drugs are the worst thing you can do. Cannabis is often classed as a drug with no harmful effects, but that simply is not proven. Academics such as Professor Wayne Hall have carried out significant research that has shown links to depression, schizophrenia, and even increased motor vehicle crashes.[86] Trying to run a business 'under the influence' will only lead to a cycle of tasks and activities that are never completed. You will lose a sense of time and remember: time is your greatest asset, you cannot get it back.

Illegal drugs also have a way of isolating you from 'normal' people and, when socialising, you will tend to gravitate towards other users. You are going to need to be in tip-top mental and physical condition to deal with the forthcoming challenges. Give yourself a fighting chance with a clear head.

---

[86] Prof Wayne Hall, Adverse health effects of non-medical cannabis use, The Lancet, http://www.thelancet.com/journals/lancet/article/PIIS0140-6736(09)61037-0/fulltext

Mind, Body, and Soul

An equation was published recently that tried to predict what we need as human beings to be happy.[87] To operate effectively as a human being we need to be fundamentally happy inside. Yes, money and success are part of that happiness, but other things make us happy too:

- Relationships, partners, and physical relations
- Friends
- Family
- Giving
- Receiving

Nurture these things and you will be in a happier and better mental state to run your business; handling the many challenges you will face to reach your goals – even from zero.

Happiness = P + (5 x E) + (3 x H)

E is existence: Health, financial, stability, friendships.

H is higher orders: Self-esteem, expectations, ambitions, sense of humour.

P is personal characteristics: Outlook on life, adaptability, and resilience

It is easy to get wrapped up in achieving our goals: we may not have time to visit family or friends. If you realise from the outset that they are intrinsically linked to your happiness then you will factor in time for them. So when your business and financial goals are met you will be doubly happy!

Don't be in the position of having made it whilst losing contact with everyone in the process.

---

[87] Rothwell Carol and Cohen Pete (Happiness Report-January 2003), 'Happiness is no Laughing Matter'

Stop the Negativity

If you know any negative friends or people, I strongly suggest you distance yourself from them or cut them out altogether. I know that sounds harsh but these 'friendships' can have a huge effect on our mental wellbeing, impair your thought processes, and take up valuable time and mental resources. You will probably need to carefully assess what a real friend is.

A real friend isn't someone who agrees with everything you say, nor is it someone who always criticises or picks faults. A person also isn't a friend just because you have known them for a long time. A true friend is someone who supports you while you support them. They can be straight and honest with you and vice versa without any jealousy, competitiveness, or judgement.

As you climb to reach and achieve a lot of your goals, many of your friendships will be tested and some may break. This is to be expected.

Always be open to meeting new people; remember the example where we told five friends to tell five of their friends about our business. Imagine if you had a network of hundred or a thousand people?

Sense of Purpose

We all like to focus on the visual but the other senses are just as important. Studies have shown that smell can have a significant effect on our mood, decision making skills, and memory. In one study, different scents of seawater, peppermint, and orange were pumped into a nightclub. The revellers reported increased enjoyment and perceived increase in quality of the music over the unscented venue.[88] Ensure your premises, shop, offices, and you always smell great!

---

[88] Schifferstein HN, Talke KS, Oudshoorn DJ, Can Ambient Scent Enhance the Nightlife Experience? https://www.ncbi.nlm.nih.gov/pmc/articles/PMC3106157/

The subconscious effects on clients will be amazing; Customers will stay in your shop for longer, you'll have happier employees, happier clients, and great first impressions. A list of the some of the best liked smells include:

1) Freshly cut grass
2) Bacon (Even some veggies have been known to like the smell of bacon!)
3) Freshly baked bread
4) Coffee.
5) Chocolate

Invest in good quality smells and use them every day, not just on special occasions! (Now, where do I buy that bacon spray? Yes, it does exist.) [89]

---

[89] https://www.amazon.co.uk/Bacon-Smell-Fragrance-Sensory-Decisions/dp/B0118FAS1G

Comic Book Page 9

The negative energy and mind drug transforms Hero into an alter ego that goes on a rampage in the City Centre. Destroying buildings and ruining his reputation in the process.

Kabooom!

The mind controlled Hero sets about the destruction of the City Centre...

How can you do this to us Hero!?

Crowds shout, fists waving. The Angels look upon the situation with despair.

REPUTATION

Public Image

Your reputation is the key in your personal life and business. If your reputation is damaged, you will find it increasingly difficult to achieve any great success despite doing everything highlighted in this book. Remember, often what people really think about your business, (or you, for that matter) will not be said to your face; do not be complacent, or think you are immune from reputation damage.

Unfortunately, people are more likely to tell a friend if they have a bad experience. For us, what this means is if one customer tells five friends and these five friends tell five friends (as in the viral effect in previous chapters) of a bad experience then we could have several thousand people viewing our business in a negative light, rightly or wrongly!

The key is to be reasonable and fair with all of your customers; deal with disputes quickly but be aware, all it takes is one person to start the rot. Then, despite how good your business is, you could be fighting for your reputation. You need some ammunition to build and protect your reputation in the first instance:

1) Testimonials/references: These are key to building trust. Especially if they are from recognised bodies or individuals.

2) Reliability/stability: Show some track record. i.e. number of years trading or background experience.

3) Become a member of a trade body or organisation.

4) Talk to potential clients: Have a landline phone or physical address that they can call or visit to show that you exist. This is doubly important if you are a company based on the internet, as new websites are often treated with suspicion.

5) Look the part: Try to present all of your materials, business cards, letterheads, and website etc. in the most professional way that you can afford.

6) Press: Try to get articles or reviews in recognised magazines or newspapers. You can write a press release yourself and submit it or even hire the services of a PR company.

7) Endorsements: Have a well-known celebrity or figure be the 'face' of the company.

8) Promote <u>yourself,</u> so *you become* the face of the company.

Despite performing all of the above, as you grow your business and you increase the number of customers you deal with, the chances of negative feedback increases. These days, unfortunately for us, this can have serious effects on our business if the negative feedback comes through social media or the internet.

Companies such as Google very rarely delete content from their database, one negative comment from a disgruntled customer or competitor can have serious effects, even if untrue.

You should make it part of your routine to check what people are saying about your company on the internet. Keep a close eye on this, especially if you are doing a lot of emailing, cold calling, or mailing to generate leads. These days most people do a quick 'Google' on anyone new they are dealing with so keep an eye on what comes up when you Google your name or company name.

Fix Up Look Sharp

If there is anything negative reported on the search engines, you need to fix it fast; whether it is true or not. It could be costing you hundreds, if not thousands, of pounds in lost business and reputation. There are various things you can do to tackle negative feedback on the search engines:

1) Post information on your own blogs. Your own blogs are rated highly by Google. So it should be high up the listings if you use your company name as the keyword in setting up your blog post. Ensure you update your blog regularly to keep it positioned high.

2) Search engine optimisation (SEO). Optimise your site for your company name. These should rank higher than other negative sites and have the effect of pushing them down in the listings. Once off the first page they are practically invisible as most people will not search past the first page of results.

3) Get customers to send feedback and post positive feedback on your site.

4) Start your own moderated web forum. The comments from these will rank highly.

5) Get more sites linked to you; these will appear in the listings when searching for your company name.

6) Contact the webmaster of the negative content and ask politely to remove any negative content. Be careful not to reply to the post itself as this may create more links to the negative post and move it up the rankings. Contact the webmaster directly.

7) Do some PR (Public relations) to raise your profile and credibility.

If you have contacted the webmaster and they will not remove the comments, you will have to register and make a reply refuting the claims or give an explanation. Remember you are in a public arena so try to avoid being emotional in your wording: Try firm but business like. View this problem as a challenge that could potentially bring more customers and publicity to your business if handled correctly. Leave a contact number so anyone viewing the negative post can contact you directly for information or reassurance.

If you are unlucky, and get negative press in magazines or newspapers, this can be doubly harmful as most newspapers have online versions as well that will almost never be deleted from Google, even if untrue. You may then need the professional help of an online reputation management company. Unfortunately, the internet is in the most part unregulated, which means anyone can post libellous, negative, or plain untrue comments. Competitors may even do this to gain market share, so be aware. Part of being successful is dealing with criticism and scrutiny; get to grips with your reputation early on.

Problem Solving:

Once you have established a good reputation or a recognised brand, you may be confronted with the problem of how to protect that reputation or brand? I wrote earlier about my experiences with the title of this book that was disputed by the largest entertainment and media company in the world; Marvel and DC Entertainments Inc, all because of the word 'Superhero'. It's a sad fact that often you can spend a fair bit of money creating, designing, and promoting a brand only for a third party to come forward claiming that you are infringing, or worse blatantly utilising a similar brand name or product to yours which you have created. So how do you protect your brand then?

The first step is to ensure you understand what you are protecting. There are different solutions available depending on what you are trying to protect. These are all grouped under Intellectual Property or IP.

Trade Mark.

If you are trying to protect a unique company name, a product name, or some kind of brand name or sign then you will need to protect it via a trade mark.[90] It is important to understand that simply registering your company name with Companies House or registering a domain name does not give you exclusive rights to that name.

Patent.

If you are trying to protect some kind of unique invention then you will need to protect it via a patent.[91]

---

[90] https://www.gov.uk/how-to-register-a-trade-mark/what-you-can-and-cant-register
[91] https://www.gov.uk/patent-your-invention

Design.

If you are looking to protect a unique design, you will need to register a design.[92] This will help you defend the shape, appearance, and layout of your design.

Copyright.

If you are trying to protect a unique creative work, such as a play, song, or music then you will need to protect it via copyright.[93] Protection via copyright is automatic; you can indicate protection by placing the symbol © and the year your work was made. The issue becomes proving that you are the original creator of the works should there be a dispute as there is no register of copyrighted works. There are bodies such as the PRS (Performing Rights Society)[94] that can be used to register musical works and would possibly help when dealing with disputes. However, it is important to understand that they do not create copyright in themselves. The best methods of proof would be to send a registered and unopened copy of the work to yourself or to lodge a copy with your bank or solicitor. Obviously, if you send a copy to yourself and there is a dispute, you would have to prove you did not swap any contents later.

Protecting your Brand or Invention.

Once you know what you are protecting, go ahead and register your brand or invention, there are different methods of protection depending on the type of Intellectual Property. As stated above, if it is a creative work there is no official registration, but there are bodies that will register your works, which could possibly help should there be a dispute.

---

[92] https://www.gov.uk/register-a-design
[93] https://www.gov.uk/copyright
[94] http://www.prsformusic.com/Pages/default.aspx

Registering a Trade Mark.

The first step in registering your trade mark, is searching the register to ensure the mark is not in use already. If it is, and you proceed with registration, the mark will be rejected. Registration can be made online at the Intellectual Property website.[95] Costs range from £170- £200 at the time of writing, plus £50 for each additional 'class' you register (category of goods, such as Food, publications, toys, etc.) The process will take up to two months but could take longer if your application is opposed by a third party. Once registered, you can place the symbol ® on your mark indicating that it is a registered mark and is protected. The rules governing trade marks are stipulated in the Trade Mark Act 1994[96], a person would have infringed on your trade mark if their sign is identical or similar enough to create confusion from the point of view of the consumer.[97] I had to utilise this Act heavily in my dispute with Marvel and DC Ent Inc. Although the registration process is relatively straightforward and can potentially be carried out by yourself, it may be wise to consult a professional prior to proceeding, since matters can get complicated if your mark is opposed.

Trade Mark dispute – How Did I Do It?

Tackling probably the largest media and entertainment company in the world was not easy and certainly not wise under normal circumstances! The full details of which are way too long and outside of the scope of this book. However, here are a few pointers on the arguments I used: My main defence was that the opponent's trade mark SUPER HEROES was a generic term (A term that had become common in everyday use).

---

[95] https://www.gov.uk/how-to-register-a-trade-mark/apply
[96] Trade Mark Act 1994
[97] s10 ibid

I utilised an American case I found to highlight the effect of trade marks becoming generic Haughton Elevator Co. v. Seeberger, 85 U.S.P.Q. 80 (1950)[98], in this case, the court held that the trademark 'ELEVATOR', then owned by Seeberger who worked for Otis (a manufacturer of moving platforms or 'Elevators'), was generic and that "it had become recognised by the general public as the name for a moving stairway and not the source of the goods" (i.e. the ESCALATOR of Otis Elevator). I argued that in a similar way SUPER HEROES had become common in everyday language and was not an indication of the source of origin of Marvel & DC's products.

I found another case: Apple, Inc. v. Amazon.com Inc., Case No. CV 11-01327 PJH (N.D. Cal. July 6, 2011)[99] in this case Apple, the well-known mobile phone manufacturer, attempted to prevent Amazon.com using the name 'APP STORE' in the course of its business. Amazon argued that the word 'App Store' was generic and 'Application Stores' were common online. The word is used by many companies to describe the service for downloading software or 'Apps' from the internet. Apple later dropped its case which is exactly what happened in my case with Marvel and DC!

I also called upon the *Trade Mark Act 1994*, in particular, s3[100] which is absolute grounds for refusal of registration. I argued that SUPER HEROES potentially should not have been registered in the first instance by Marvel and DC.

S3(1)(b) Signs which are devoid of distinctive character – (The trade mark was not distinctive enough – others used the term superhero to describe their characters).

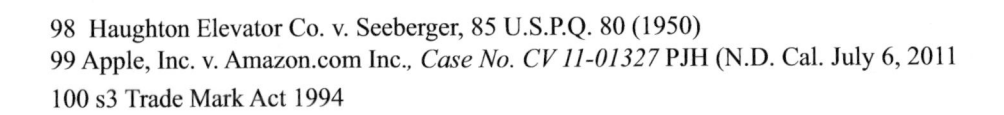

---

98 Haughton Elevator Co. v. Seeberger, 85 U.S.P.Q. 80 (1950)
99 Apple, Inc. v. Amazon.com Inc., *Case No. CV 11-01327* PJH (N.D. Cal. July 6, 2011
100 s3 Trade Mark Act 1994

S3(1)(c) trade marks which consist exclusively of signs or indications which may serve, in trade, to designate the kind, quality, quantity, intended purpose, value, geographical origin, the time of production of goods or rendering of services, or other characteristics of goods or services. (In my opinion, within the creative industries, superheroes was a term used in the trade of creative writing).

S3(1)(d) trade marks which consist exclusively of signs or indications which have become <u>customary in the current language</u> or in the bona fide and established practices of the trade.[101] *(Superheroes, in my opinion, had become commonplace in every day language).*

I also argued that my trade mark was distinct from the opponent's mark in that it consisted of three separate words (ZERO TO SUPERHERO), whereas the opponent's mark consisted of two. I also argued the opponent's mark SUPER HEROES had been commonly used by other parties that were not controlled by the opponent as well as giving examples.

Marvel subsequently dropped the case, and I continued to register Zero To Superhero®, officially!

Registering a Patent.

Similar to registering a trade mark, the first step in registering your unique invention is searching the register to ensure there is nothing similar already registered via the Online Patent Information and Document Inspection Service.[102]

---

[101] Trade Mark Act 1994
[102] https://www.ipo.gov.uk/p-ipsum.htm

Unfortunately, registration of a patent is much more expensive and complicated than registering a trade mark. The intellectual property office website indicates that only one in twenty people get a patent without professional help. Applications can cost several thousands of pounds with professional help and can take up to five years. If you wish to apply yourself, you can,[103] however you are best advised to seek the help of a professional.

Registering a Design.

If you have a unique design, you can protect it by registering it at the Intellectual Property Office.[104] You will need to provide illustrations of your design and the fees can range from £50 for one design to £150 for up to fifty designs. Registering your design will protect it for up to twenty-five years.

Domain names

As mentioned earlier, registering a domain name does not automatically protect your brand should someone else utilise that name as a company name or brand name, you should always register your brand as a trade mark.However, what if someone uses a domain name that is confusingly similar to your own website or your domain expires and is picked up by someone else? Domain names are often hotly disputed in this internet age and the organisation that handles UK disputes is Nominet.[105] Nominet provides an initial free dispute resolution service; should there not be any resolution, there will be a fee of up to £750 for an expert and binding decision on the matter. If the decision is in your favour, the other party will have to transfer the domain to yourself or stop using it.

---

[103] https://www.ipo.gov.uk/p-apply-before.htm
[104] https://www.gov.uk/apply-register-design
[105] https://www.nominet.uk/domains/resolving-uk-domain-disputes-and-complaints/

Non-Disclosure Agreements (NDA's).

Non-disclosure agreements are handy if you want to keep your ideas, processes, or inventions secret when you conduct meetings with others such as investors, business coaches, mentors, or banks etc. The problem with NDA's is they are difficult to enforce, and some will not sign them. It is important to remember that if you do not tell anyone your unique information, you are guaranteed to keep it confidential.

Conclusion:

So there you have it. You should ensure that you trade mark, patent, or register any brands, designs, or intellectual property that you create. This way you can legally prevent others from using them. If you are going to talk to anyone about trade secrets, you should consider non-disclosure agreements.

Remember that registering a domain name or company name does not automatically prevent others from using that name, you should in addition register a trade mark. Should there be a dispute with domain names, you can approach Nominet for dispute resolution.

SEARCH ENGINES

Comic Book Page 10

"I need to find the mind altered Hero.."

Unlimited Hero tries to locate Hero, now altered by the negative energy and mind drug.

Unlimited Hero uses robotic spiders that scour the city in search of Hero. The robotic spiders click into action...

Click, click click

The robotic spiders send a map location to Unlimited Hero.

"I will destroy this city with my Weather Machine and take rule from the Angels.."

"And then I will destroy Hero!"

Mind altered Hero and Mort are in the City Centre Park, where Dr Mort intends to destroy Hero and the entire city with a new deadly device. THE WEATHER MACHINE.

SEARCH ENGINE OPTIMISATION

Search for The Hero

We spoke in the last chapter about using search engine optimisation (SEO) to fight against negative feedback. SEO is critical if you want any success on the web and wish to get registered in Google. So, how do you get your brand new website listed and searchable so that people can find you?

I met an SEO expert at a business meetup; this is what search engine expert Alexander Aranda[106] says:

'*Search engine optimisation, or as it is more commonly known, SEO, is the process of making your site more visible, credible, and trustworthy amongst search engines. As search engines become more sophisticated and good at evaluating good quality sites, users also equate that quality directly with your website.*

The Three Point Triangular Approach™

In my Three Point Triangular Approach™ *I have developed an approach that allows me to quickly analyse and deal with any search engine optimisation challenge. This approach breaks down SEO into three distinct areas: Content, accessibility, usefulness.*

Top tip for each area:
Content: Make sure that your content is unique, something that cannot be found anywhere else.
Accessibility: Ensure that you have an effective navigation system that allows users to reach your content quickly and easily.

Usefulness: Your content should be useful to your target audience! '

Alexender Aranda
SEO Expert

---

[106] http://www.alexanderaranda.com/about

There are three more practical things you must do to optimise your website. You need to do these three things to get the best from your new site:

1) Ensure the code on your site (HTML)[107] is optimised. To do this you need to ensure your website page AND its code contains the required keyword(s). For example, you have a website that sells mp3 players soyour main keywords may be 'mp3 players for sale'. You should try and imagine what your potential customers will type into the search engine to pick your keywords.

To fully optimise your site the TITLE line in your website code should contain the keyword or the main elements of the keyword e.g.: TITLE = 'mp3 player for sale'.

The keyword line should contain all of your keywords e.g.: KEYWORD = 'mp3 players for sale, mp3 players, new mp3 players'.

The actual written text in the website should contain your keywords.

You should also ensure the DESCRIPTION line contains elements that potential customers might type into search engines.

---

[107] Hypertext Mark-up Language

For an example of this layout, go to http://www.grahamjules.co.uk, right click on the page, and select "View source" (Internet Explorer). You will then be able to see the HTML for my website. You can see at the top of the page the three tags discussed:

```
<title>Graham Jules AKA Jules</title>
<meta name="description" content="Graham Jules, company director, entrepreneur, author of Business Zero To Superhero, music producer Blam Records 1992-1998. G.Jules" />
<meta name="keywords" content="graham jules, jules, blam productions, g jules, zero to superhero, new art originals, real world gallery, business zero to superhero" />
```

Tips: Each page on your website should be optimised differently; for example, if you also sell CD players, you could optimise another page for the keyword 'CD players' etc.

Do not overuse the keyword in your website or you may be penalised by the search engine for spamming.

Do not optimise too many keywords on a single page or your results will be diluted; choose one or two keywords per page and build on them.

You may need to do some 'keyword research' to pick suitable keywords. It will be difficult to rank highly for very popular keywords: Try and make your keywords more specific. For example, you have a shop that sells mp3 players in London. Rather than using the keywords 'mp3 players for sale', you could use the keywords 'mp3 player for sale London'. It will be easier for your site to rank higher up the listings as you are excluding all those searches not specific to London. Remember to optimise for keywords that generate enquiries/leads and more importantly, sales!

2) You need to get one-way links <u>to</u> your website of suitable page ranking.

Page ranking is a system Google uses to rate a website. The higher Google rates a website, the higher the ranking. The lowest is 0 and the highest is 10. Your goal should be to get links pointing to your site from high PR sites; the more one-way links you get from high PR sites, the more important your own site will appear to Google and you will move up the listings for your keyword. For example, you place a link on a high PR (5) site for your web page selling mp3 players. The link should contain your keyword in the text e.g.: 'mp3 players for sale'. When the visitor clicks on this link they will be taken to your optimised page.

Place your optimised link on as many high PR third party sites as possible to improve your ranking in Google. This is a lengthy process but it WORKS! You will need to contact the web master of the third party sites and ask for your link to be included; try and choose sites that are related to your site in some way to increase the relevance and effectiveness of your SEO.

Do not use link farms or other bulk link creating services. Your website may be penalised. Always build your links slowly, you want your links to appear as natural as possible.

3) You need to get your website crawled by the search bots or Web spider.

The Web spider is a software code that scans all the websites on the internet (crawls) and saves them in the search engine's database. You will not appear in the search engine when someone types in your keyword until your website has been crawled. To get your website crawled, register with that search engine. If you have already linked to a high PR site, Google should find you automatically. If you have no inbound links, you will have to get crawled manually. To get your website crawled, register with the search engine and submit your website.

If you have another site or know someone with a website already on the search engine database, you should link to your new site so the search engines can crawl you quickly. Once in the database there is no need to submit again. There are certain search engines, such as Yahoo, that charge for submission at the time of writing this book, although the majority are free.

Once you have done these three things, your website will start to appear in the results of search engines. Of course, there is a lot more to SEO than this, however that is beyond the scope of this book. These topics were the essentials that will get you started; you can find out much more information on the subject through specialist books to help you turbo-charge your website to the first page or number one in the listings!

Tips: You can use services/software that submit your site to hundreds of search engines/directories. However, there is no need to do this more than once and you should not need to pay any subscription fees.

If you are not web savvy, or do not have the time, you can employ a SEO company to optimise your website, source the high PR websites, and place your links there. Be careful and ensure that they are using reputable sites in line with your industry or you could be penalised. Using a SEO company can save you hours of time and, as we know, our time is very precious.

> Using a SEO company can save you hours of time and, as we know, our time is very precious.

Press to Play

While we are trying to increase our rankings in the search engines, it is easy to obsess over our search positions and forget about the big picture; always try to keep in mind that the internet is only one form of media outlet, albeit an important one. We can take advantage of some of the other available media including:

1) Print media (magazines, newspapers etc.)
2) Radio
3) TV

Is that not expensive? I hear you ask. Yes, it can be if you advertise; however, if you approach it correctly you can get free coverage from these often forgotten about media outlets in this increasingly digital age.

So how do we go about getting a piece of the action and grabbing some of the free press attention we need to catapult our business forward? Well, the answer lies in creating what's called a 'Press Release' and sending it to the relevant editors of media in your field. A press release should be an interesting, factual piece of writing with an attention grabbing headline. Try not to make your press release too 'salesy' or just another extension of your website. Remember, it needs to grab attention and be of interest to someone who has never heard of your company before.

Some easy ways to create an interesting press release are to host an interesting event to launch your product or to conduct market research that gives some interesting results for your industry and then to write about that. As an example, if you are providing a service in computers and your research finds that 90% of under-12s are computer literate, that could be newsworthy. Whereas, 'we are the best computer services company in the world' will probably not be that interesting news wise. Always keep in mind the reader of your press release and study news articles both in and outside your industry for ideas.

So now you've got an idea for a press release but how should it be formatted and what should it contain? There are no hard and fast rules but the basics are:

1) Headline. This should be attention grabbing, short, and memorable.

2) Say when you want your press release published. This is especially important if you have a time-critical event or product launch. Include the words 'for immediate release' at the top of the page if your release is not bound by a specific date.

3) In your first paragraph, include the five 'Ws and H': who, what, where, when, why and how. This will give your reader an immediate summary of what you are selling.

4) At the end of your release include the word 'Ends' or ### in bold. This tells the editor that anything after this point is not to be included in the press release and should not be published.

5) Remember to include your contact details, including direct phone number and web address, so you can be contacted for interview if necessary. If you do not want these to be published, place these details after 'Ends'.

6) Keep it short, no more than one page.

Once you have crafted your release, send it to your desired media outlets via email. If emailing your press release, remember to include your headline in the subject and not just type 'Press Release'. Research and target your press release to the media outlets that fit with your industry sector or story; you can find the names of newspaper editors on their website or in back copies of their publications. Ensure you send the press release to the correct person, do not blast the entire newspaper with anything you may send.

Do not add large attachments to your email or it probably will not be read. If you have images that relate to your story, include them in the body of the email but do not use high-resolution files that take up loads of space. The journalist can always ask for high-resolution images, if they are interested.

It is often much easier to get coverage in your local press. You should target these first and then branch out to specialist press or consumer press. Then, if you have a very interesting story, the national press. Remember to follow up on your release but don't be too pushy. Don't forget radio and TV.

The advantages of getting press coverage in this way are increased profile, visibility, and trust from your readership or listeners. Remember, it has not cost you a penny! Most media outlets have websites and if you have also been included in their website this is free SEO! To maximise your coverage, make sure to include your press coverage in your website or blog with links to the media outlets covering you. If you have included your web address in your press release and that is then published, you could see your visitors increase overnight.

There are numerous public relations (PR) websites that you can submit your release to such as PRweb.com and Prfire.com. You can use these to broadcast your release online and increase SEO even further. You may find initially that your press release efforts are limited and you may not get much coverage. If that is the case and once you have some budget, you can turbo-charge your efforts by hiring a PR company with good contacts in your industry.

Once again, ensure you have a reason to splash out further on PR by testing your own PR campaign for free first. Once you have verified your newsworthiness, go for it!

AUTOMATION

Comic Book Page 11

"I'm gonna need some backup, I'll use these quantum robots to fight Dr Mort."

Unlimited Hero is prepared, he has created an army of quantum automated robots.

Vroom BOOM!

"They can appear in many places at once and overpower Mort."

"I command you automated robots, appear!"

Bzzz

The automated robots battle with Doctor Mort and mind altered Hero. Dr Mort sends a brain wave to his evil Weather Machine…

Kpowwwww!

The Weather Machine comes to life. A fiery flame shoots from the sky.

AUTOMATION

Automation Baby

Automation is key to growing a *good* business into a *great* business. Remember, our goal is to be making money while we are sleeping, so to achieve this, automation is key.

Remember, automation does not always mean technical equipment. It could mean staff or outsourcing to perform repetitive tasks in greater volume.

Example: While developing your marketing strategy, sending 5,000 email pitches to your clients generated £2,000 in sales.

To automate the process, you:

1) Build a website to take orders.
2) Buy a mailing list and generate 5,000 email leads a month.
3) Outsource to an email marketing company who send your pitch to the 5,000 leads a month, and who visit and order directly on your website.

You can see how this system is automated and will continue to provide leads and customers, market willing, forever; even while we are sleeping, without you hardly doing a thing.

The beauty of automation is that if you want to increase revenue you can, simply by increasing your leads or by increasing your conversion rate. Obviously it will cost to put a system in place, but once in place, it should pay for itself, as long as you have done your homework. Remember, this is just an example; all businesses can be automated to some extent. You should be looking to automate repetitive tasks from the outset to preserve your valuable time and to turbo-charge and 'scale' your business.

Ways to automate:

1) Automation software. You can automate repetitive, everyday computer tasks with software.

2) Staff. Employ staff to carry out tasks you do not have the time to do yourself.

3) Outsourcing. Remember, all outsourcing means is paying another company to do the dirty work, which means more time for you! (And your business.) Why spend hours typing figures into spreadsheets when there's a company that will do it for a reasonable rate in a faster time? Remember, your time is valuable. Outsource as soon as you can. Do not be trapped into 'job mode'. Hours spent working does not mean more money earned. We've proved it!

4) Custom system: Development of custom equipment and software can be expensive. But once again, if you have done your homework you should know the pros and cons from the outset. If you can create an automated system to create or deliver a service, your sales could sky-rocket.

The whole point of automating the business is scalability. Remember our equation:

Paid customers = number of leads x conversion rate

With automation in place, we can increase our marketing spend knowing our paid customers should increase without much
extra effort on our part! Once we are in this position and if we have a good market and demand, the sky is the limit - marketing budget allowing.

Think of all the multi-million pound businesses. Think of all the systems they have in place, whether it's:

- Software
- Packaging equipment
- Call handling
- Bottling, canning equipment
- Manufacturing equipment

Without automation it would be impossible to fulfil the demand. Automation has the added benefit that once in place, it is cheaper than an ad hoc system. You can pass the savings to the customer or keep as profits! So, why not do it?

Licence To Thrill

As discussed, automation is key. If you find yourself doing the same things over and over, and your turnover remains the same year after year, it may be time to automate to boost your revenue.

Another way to do this would be to license or franchise your product or service. When you do this, you give rights to an individual or company to carry out business using the business name and procedures. They would operate in a different region or territory from you to avoid conflicts. The good news is as the licensor or franchisor, you will get a slice of the turnover, not just the profits!

INCREASE PROFIT OVERNIGHT

Profit Prophet

There are a few simple ways you can increase your turnover and profit overnight! Yes, really!

1) Increase your prices. Yes, it sounds obvious, but don't be afraid to increase your prices by a few per cent a year. After all, as your costs are probably increasing, so should your prices. Remember, if you are marketing your services on price alone, you could be on a slippery slope, so ensure you are not making the mistake of just trying to be the cheapest.

2) Ask for referrals. Contact your client list and ask them to recommend someone. Automate the referral process and ask after each sale or order.

3) Discounts. Have a discount or promotion. Always ensure it is *time limited* to maximise effectiveness.

4) Up-sell the customer. This is powerful. Get your client to buy from you twice rather than once. As an example, a client buys a painting from your shop. Why not offer a frame or picture hooks at the point of sale. If you can automate your up-sell, it can be very powerful. Online, your website could offer an up-sell when an order is placed. Remember, once someone has bought, they are more likely to buy again, so get that sale in right away! Increase your turnover and profit by up-selling.

5) Target your best clients and offer them a premium package.

6) Increase your leads/marketing. Generate more leads and, as we've seen, your sales will increase.

7) Improve your conversion rate. Target your sales pitch to the right people. Perfect the wording and appearance of your pitch and fine-tune until your conversion rate increases.

Up-sell the customer. This is powerful. Get your client to buy from you twice rather than once. As an example, a client buys a painting from your shop. Why not offer a frame or picture hooks at the point of sale. If you can automate your up-sell, it can be very powerful.

GOOGLE

Like An Ever Flowing Stream

Google offers a number of packages as well as searches to enhance your business. One of those is AdSense. AdSense can be found at: http://www.google.com/adsense.

What AdSense allows you to do is to get paid every time someone visits your website and clicks on any Google ads! If you have a high number of visitors to your website, this can be a free additional stream of income! Once set up, you will not have to do anything – just let the cash roll in!

You get paid according to the ad type, usually a few pence per click. Once you reach a threshold ($100), Google will send you a cheque or transfer your revenue that month. Many sites make good income from this model alone. Since it is free, there is nothing to lose in signing up and incorporating Google's ad code into your website.

Back On The Map

Google Places for Business (Now called Google My Business) is another free service that literally allows you to place your business on the map (Google Maps). This is great if you have a physical space such as a shop or other location. When a potential customer searches for your service in your area, your business will appear on Google Maps and also high up in the search results. To register just go to: https://www.google.com/business/ .

When you register, ensure you fill in as much information as possible about your business, including pictures and video, if you have any. (You can even upload a 3D virtual tour of your business.) Also, if you have multiple locations, create different locations within Google My Business. Google My Business will help your website be seen higher up in the search engines and add credibility. Clients can see at a glance that you exist and have a fixed location. This service is a valuable extension to your own company website. You can even set up special offers and discounts via the interface to give to your Google My Business site visitors.

You can also view what potential customers are searching for and where they are coming from. They can also leave feedback and comments which can be viewed in the search results. So, this could also be used as a tool to enhance your leads/keywords.

Word Up

AdWords Express is probably one of Google's better-known services. It enables you to advertise your business via paid ads that will appear alongside the natural search results. The way it works is you pay a fee each time someone clicks on your ad (pay per click). Each click will cost from a few pence to several pounds. You choose which keywords will trigger the ad and you set a bid price for each keyword. You can also set an overall budget. The more you have to spend, the more your ad will be shown. AdWords can be found at: http://www.google.com/adwords

The benefits of AdWords are obvious. When someone searches your keywords, for example: 'mp3 players for sale', your ad will be shown alongside the natural search results, meaning you can launch your product immediately without having to wait months for SEO to work. The last few years has seen tremendous growth in these areas; there are now other players in the field that may be relevant to your business, such as Facebook[108], YouTube[109], Instagram[110], Twitter[111], Snapchat[112], etc. But be *very* careful to set suitable budgets as you could find you waste valuable resources on thousands of clicks that amount to no sales!

As always with any marketing campaign, ensure you test first before you splash out big time on AdWords. AdWords is not a quick fix, so test, test, test to ensure it is right for your business.

---

[108] https://www.facebook.com/business/
[109] https://www.youtube.com/yt/advertise/en-GB/
[110] https://business.instagram.com/advertising?locale=en_GB
[111] https://ads.twitter.com/login
[112] https://www.snapchat.com/l/en-gb/ads

KEEPING RECORDS

Paper, Scissors, Stone

When starting your business, ensure you keep all your paperwork in good order. Yes, I know it's boring, but once you start making money, if you haven't kept your files up to date, you may be caught between a rock and a hard place. You will need to prove:

1) Where it comes from.
2) What you spent it on.

The only way you can do this is by keeping adequate records and keeping the evidence. These records are going to be crucial should you wish to attract investors or expand your business, so invest in some A4 box files right away.

What records to keep:
1) Keep all your receipts. Get into the habit of keeping every receipt. I throw them into a large envelope once a month and sort the three envelopes quarterly.

2) Keep a record of your sales. I have a spreadsheet that includes all cash purchases, bank purchases, and sales. You don't need anything too complicated. If you are VAT registered, you will need to do this so you can calculate and submit your VAT return. Try to keep on top of this, monthly or quarterly is fine. Ensure you include all transactions from bank statements as well as cash receipts.

3) Keep all your bank statements, both business AND personal. *Never* throw away your bank statements. I know you can get them online these days, but depending on your bank, they may only store 12–24 months, so you may get stuck if you need to prove something earlier than that. You could be forced to pay £5–£10 a page for a duplicate bank statement with some banks!

4) Do annual accounts. Get your annual accounts done by a recognised accountant. This need not be expensive, there are many operating online at reasonable rates. Also, get them to do your company tax return if you are a limited company.

5) Keep an eye on your credit file, both business and personal. Your credit file is important for obvious reasons. Keep an eye on it and check your file every 6–12

months and save a copy on file.

6) Keep all correspondence from banks, customers, enquiry letters, emails, suppliers etc. Keep it all and file it in a box file. If there is a dispute you will be glad you kept that letter from two years back.

7) Obey the law. By law, a limited company must file accounts annually and keep records for up to three years or six years for a public company,[113] so you need to do this to stay on the right side of the law.

Ensure you keep proper accounts from the *beginning*. Do not skip on this or you will regret it later. Your accounts are the only way a potential investor, bank, or even potential customer can tell you are a genuine business worth taking seriously. Ensure you do your accounts and if you are a limited company, ensure you file them with Companies House or you will be fined.

Remember, if you are a limited company, your accounts are available online for anyone to download as they are in the public domain! If you keep good accounts, submit them on time; the doors will be open to investors, and bank loans for future expansion. You will add credibility to your business and attract better clients and suppliers. In the past, I have researched potential clients only to find a dormant limited company - instant credibility lost forever. Do not let this be you, keep your company records up to date.

---

[113] Section 388 Companies Act 2006

Remember, if you are a limited company, your accounts are available online for anyone to download as they are in the public domain!

RISK

Comic Book Page 12

Hero is injected with positive energy by Unlimited.

Zzzppppp

The automated robots deflect the Weather Machine by using quantum energy. They banish the almighty weather system to an alternate reality.

Nooo, problem!

Thanks Unlimited

Ugggh..

BLAAAM!

Now lets finish Dr Mort!...

Hero captures Doctor Mort and imprisons him in the City Of Angels in a crystal prison..

Noooooooo!

174

RISK

Risky Business

Business is about taking risks, but there are certain risks you should not take. Imagine you've spent your start-up capital setting up your small office, and one day you turn your key in the door and the whole place is flooded! You could be back to square one in seconds, and depending how long it took to get your start-up capital together, this could set you back a number of years.

You could be affected by a flood, burglary, or fire. Remember when you start/buy something new to insure against its loss! For a few pounds a month you could be saving yourself from business disaster.

It happened to me. I had expanded the music business with a brand new PA system for £1,000 for a rehearsal room. I installed the system in the new space and had not placed the system on the insurance schedule. The next day, there was a break-in and £1,000 gone, just like that. Don't let it happen to you. Insure against these unforeseen risks – it's worth it.

If you are employing anyone or are open to the public you will need:

1) Employers Liability Insurance.[114]
2) Public Liability Insurance.

Employers liability insurance is compulsory, public liability insurance is not. This cover is required to protect you from anyone injuring themselves – either an employee or the public using your products or service. You will need to display the provided certificates at your premises. Do not forget these either because if the worst happens, you could be out of business or face a huge bill. Ouch.

Of course, you should shop around for the best possible deal as insurance prices vary greatly.

While we are on the subject of not taking undue risks, ensure you have covered yourself legally when it comes to arrangements with your customers and

---

[114] Employers' Liability (Compulsory Insurance) Act 1969

suppliers. Consider having written agreements (contracts) for ALL of your dealings. Yes, I know it's boring and getting the signed documents can delay deals, but do not skip this!

If you are trading on the web, you will need to implement online terms and conditions that can be accepted by your customers. If you are providing goods online or by mail order, you will need to be aware of laws such as Distance Selling Regulations[115] that give your customers the right to return goods within a seven-day time period, no questions asked.

If you are hiring or renting anything to a customer, consider taking proof of ID so you know exactly who you are dealing with. If you are providing services and you are paid after the event, ensure you take a deposit and have terms and conditions in place, so if your client cancels or is late paying, you are both aware of the consequences.

Unfortunately these days, disputes are part and parcel of running a business. While the majority of people are honest and straightforward, every once in a while you will come across a client, supplier, or even an employee who will dispute any agreements you have and will deny all knowledge to avoid payment or responsibility. Make sure you have written agreements in place to cover yourself.

You must ensure you are fully up to date on the law with regard to your individual business. Many businesses require licences or special qualifications to operate. You need to talk to a professional who understands the law and the consequences for your venture. You don't want to end up with the situation of starting your venture and finding out you are breaking the law or end up being fined or sued.

Do not get caught out and deal with a client or supplier without an agreement. If there is a problem, it could end up costing you a lot of money. If you cannot afford to get legal documents drafted, a signed letter or email confirmation of your terms is better than nothing at all. If your business is high-risk, consider taking out business insurance to cover you against any future legal claims.

---

[115] The Consumer Contracts (Information, Cancellation and Additional Charges) Regulations 2013

SAVING/INVESTING

Saving Grace

In order to be truly successful, it is important to change your mindset as far as money is concerned.

Money is a tool and should be used as such. Get used to putting a small amount, say 5–10%, away in a separate savings account. You should do this monthly automatically. This can be your contingency fund for emergencies. Once you have enough in your fund to cover two to three months' overheads, you should put any additional cash into investments.

There is no point in amassing or leaving cash sitting in an account earning hardly any interest. You need your cash out there working and providing cash flow. If you think about it, money sitting in an account will actually lose value each year if inflation is greater than your savings interest rate. You need to invest your spare cash so it outstrips inflation and grows year on year.

Investments that usually rise long-term are:

1) Property
2) Shares

If you place your spare cash into property and shares, over the long term your money should increase in value. Of course, over the short term you could lose money.

Don't think that you need a lot of money to start investing in shares or property. Some banks have share dealing plans where you can buy into shares for as little as £20 a month. You should choose reliable shares that have performed year on year. Also, do not think you cannot afford current house prices. Remember, there are all kinds and price bands of property, both here in the UK and abroad, both residential and commercial. If you think outside of the box, you can still get bargains.

You should continue investing rather than saving alongside your regular business. This could provide additional income and meets our criteria of making money while we sleep!

Remember to invest in *actual shares* and not just spread betting, which is a form of speculation using credit (or margin), which is quite risky – you can lose more money than you put in. If your investment in shares rises, you could wake up one morning to a cash bonus. Not a bad way to start the day! If the company pays dividends you should also receive a payment per share held annually. If you decide to let out your property investments via a good agent, you will receive regular payments while you expend little energy or time on the portfolio.

Many successful entrepreneurs invest in start-ups themselves. So, if you have some extra cash, you could place it into successful entrepreneurs of the future. These days, sites such as Angel list, Seedrs etc., make this relatively straightforward to do, but bear in mind that returns could be non-existent or very minimal, and substantial risk is involved in this type of investing.

The earlier you start investing rather than just saving, the better. So start your investment plan today!

Investing thought: Compound interest is king!

If you could invest just £1 a day (£30 a month) with a growth rate of 8% per annum compounded, it would be worth £145,101 after 45 years or £693,488 after 60 years of compound interest. Compound interest in simple terms is earning interest on your original capital *and* any interest earned. It may take a while but compound interest can add up to serious cash over time.

If you could invest just £1 a day (£30 a month) with a growth rate of 8% per annum compounded, it would be worth £145,101 after 45 years or £693,488 after 60 years of compound interest.

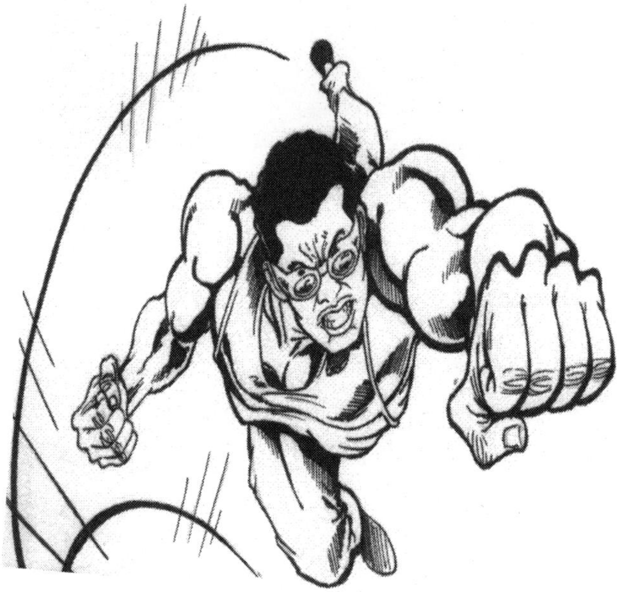

HOW TO FIND INVESTORS

Comic Book Page 13

Hero and Unlimited Hero receive accolades from the Angels on a large stage in the City of Angels. There are crowds of people gathered.

Hurrah! Hero!

Hurrah! Hero!

Hero, we imbue you with additional special powers..

182

HOW TO FIND INVESTORS

City Of Angels

Once you have gained some 'traction' or some paying customers and are generating regular turnover, you may want to raise some funds to expand and turbo-charge your business! There are a number of ways to raise funds and tap into investors and all of these options should be available in most major cities:

1) Angel Investors
2) Venture Capital
3) Stock market float. Initial public offering (IPO)

There are pros and cons for each of the methods.

A) Angel Investors

Pros:
1) They will invest £5,000 – £250,000. Angel investors are often entrepreneurs who have done it before, so they can also add experience to the equation. They will often invest in high-risk ventures.

2) Flexible contracts. They can invest small to medium amounts, no monthly fees or monthly repayments.

Cons:
1) They may push you to sell to realise their investment.

2) They will often not reinvest in the venture.

3) They will often want a large return on their investment – often 10–40%

4) They are hard to find!

B) Venture Capital (VC)

Pros:
1) They will invest £250,000 – £15 million. VCs often have more capital to invest than individual angels.

2) They do not want monthly repayments to repay the cash.

3) They are easy to find.

Cons:
1) They will often want (insist) on proof of concept.

2) They may take a controlling stake in your company and put in place their own management team.

3) They may push for a stock market float to realise their investment.

4) They may not even look at you unless you have been trading for at least two years.

C) Stock Market Float

Pros:
1) They will raise £1,000,000+. Great access to new capital.

2) Very large sums can be raised.

3) It increases your company profile.

4) It creates a market for your shares.

Cons:
1) Floatation costs are large. Also, on-going costs are substantial. Loads of fees! £50,000+.

2) Your business will need to show it can generate consistent profits.

3) The value of your company is at the mercy of market fluctuations.

4) Lots of red tape and regulation.

It is important that you choose the right route to realise your investment capital. Most new companies go via the angel investor route as it is more flexible. That is the route we will be looking at here. So, first things first: How do you find an angel investor?

In Search Of Angels

Angel investors are mysterious by nature, so they are very hard to track down as they do not want to be bombarded by investment opportunities. The main area to look for angel investors in this day and age is primarily the internet. There are many sites that put you in contact with investors (often for a fee). I have listed some below:

1) Crowdcube
2) Seedrs
3) Angel Investment Network.co.uk
4) Venture Giant
5) Angels Den
6) Company Partners
7) AngelList
8) Crunchbase

The fees will vary wildly from £0 to £30 monthly, up to £1,000s for a presentation opportunity.

Tread carefully and ensure you are ready or you could spend a lot of money needlessly. Personally, I do not believe in pay to pitch, so I have included a free list you can pitch to directly:

Tip: 800+ Free Investor List

I have a free list of hundreds of investor/angels/VC contacts. If you register online and upload a picture of yourself with this book you can access it.

http://www.business-zerotosuperhero.co.uk/investor-list/

You can locate details/names of investors on websites such as Angel List[116], which is a Facebook/Twitter type site that can be used to promote your investment proposal to investors. Some of these sites are better than others. Which ones you choose will depend on your business and your capital requirements. I do not endorse or recommend any of these. It's up to you to do your homework and ensure their model suits you and your business.

Don't forget LinkedIn, which is a good source of potential contacts. You can create a profile for yourself and your business and add investors as you meet them. You can also contact investors that look interesting through the site. Be careful not to spam though, or you will be blocked.

Now you know where to find them, but what do you need to do to convince them to give you the cash? The first thing you need to do is to incorporate your company if you have not done so already and run a limited company. We covered this earlier in this book.

[116] https://angel.co/

Every investor will want to see a business plan or at least a summary of one (such as a presentation deck - more about decks later).

You should complete your business plan first before trying to interest investors. If an investor is interested, you want to be able to send your plan and additional information right away without any delays. Your business plan doesn't have to be overly long and complicated; however, it should contain the following information:

1) Introduction to your company

2) Achievements so far

3) Financial performance

4) Your goals

5) The market (with statistics)

6) Your plan to make it happen

7) The marketing: How you intend to market the venture

8) Operations: Members of your team or staff that are needed to realise your goals

9) Investment: The amount you are seeking and the equity (% percentage) you are giving away. Make sure you give a realistic valuation. See 'Valuing your business' later in this chapter.

10) Your exit strategy: How will the investor get their money back?

11) Financials (summary) Years 1–3: Turnover, gross profit, net profit.

The above is fine for your summary plan. To create your full plan, you should also add the following:

1) Full financials Years 1 – 3: Cash flow forecast and profit and loss

2) Three years' accounts if already trading

3) CVs of the directors

4) List of professional advisors, accounts, lawyers, any additional information, press coverage etc.

Once you have your business plan, edit a summarised version and email/upload it to the site(s) you are using for introductions and wait for any interest. If you have created an interesting plan, you will get requests for more information. When you do, send them your full plan and any requested information.

> Your goal is to get your first investment meeting!

Take My Tip

Tips for your business plan:

1) You can evaluate your business plan using software such as D-RISK IT[117] which can be downloaded as an app or run online at http://www.drisk.it/microsite. This software will give you a fundraising 'health check'. The blurb states: *"Taking 'random' out of founder fundraising. A diagnostic deal tool for start-up founders and investors that via a series of key deal stress tests, produces reporting on investment deal readiness."*

2) Put your company logo on all pages of your plan.

3) Collate your full business plan in one PDF file to make it easier to read, especially if emailing.

4) Use pictures of your product or business in your plan.

5) Don't make it complicated. Keep it free from industry jargon. Keep it interesting.

6) Update your business plan with any feed-back you glean from potential investors. If everyone is saying the same thing, be prepared to change your plan to make it more appealing to investors.

7) Do not divulge *all* your company secrets in your plan, but give enough information to entice investors. This is particularly important if you are uploading to a public site.

8) If you are printing your plan, bind it so investors don't lose any pages.

9) Have a look at other companies' business plans on various websites. Make sure yours is as good, if not better.

10) Do the plan yourself. This is *important*, as you will need to be able to answer in-depth questions about your plan. Paying someone else to do it is probably not a good idea, as you will need to be very familiar with your plan when you eventually meet

---

[117] http://www.drisk.it

an investor. (If you really can't do it yourself, ensure you know it inside out.)

11) Be patient: It can take 6–12 months, even longer, to get any interest or investment. Approach as many investors as you can.

12) Valuing your business. If you are giving 10% of equity and you are asking for £100,000, this means you are valuing your business at £1,000,000, so be certain your business can show adequate revenue over sufficient time to justify this. A reasonable valuation is even more important if you have very few sales, or no turnover to date. Unrealistic valuations can put investors off, so ensure you can justify your figures.

13) You can use services such as DocSend[118] to share your plan or summary with potential investors. The advantage is you can password protect your plans and also get valuable data, such as page views, the amount of time spent on a page, or if your investor has viewed your plan at all!

[118] https://docsend.com

INVESTMENT MEETING

First Meeting

So, one day you will open your email and there, lying in your inbox, will be an email from your potential investor. They have just read your plan and want to meet you. You have an investment meeting! Congratulations! What now? How do you prepare for such a meeting? Don't worry; there are just a few things you need for your meeting:

1) Your presentation slides or deck: This is a Power Point presentation of your summary business plan.

2) You: The investor will want to evaluate you, so be presentable, on time, and polite.

3) Answers: Investors will want to question you about your business. Be prepared to answer loads of questions. Work out the most likely ones beforehand.

4) Business plan, business cards, and other materials.

Hit The Deck

Your deck is your PowerPoint presentation slide-show of your business plan. When you meet your investor, you need to be focused on what you are trying to present. Your deck will help you present your project professionally.

If you have never used PowerPoint before, it is really quite easy. You can create text, graphics, etc. for your slideshow and then move each slide on by pressing the space bar. Make your deck simple, colourful, and interesting. Remember, pictures tell a thousand words so include your logo, pictures, and graphs. Try not to make your presentation just reams and reams of text. Keep it short with bullet points, no long sentences.

What should be included in the deck?

Well, your deck should be a maximum of 10–15 screens long and should contain the following:

1) Screen 1: Your logo, your main strap-line, your contact details.

2) Screen 2: What you do, any achievements so far.

3) Screen 3: The directors. Brief information on those in charge (you). Their background and successes to date.

4) Screen 4: The problem. Explain the problem you are trying to solve with your venture.

5) Screen 5: The solution. Explain how you intend to solve the problem highlighted previously.

6) Screen 6: Case studies. If you have already trialled your venture or have existing customers, give examples here.

7) Screen 7: Marketing/sales. Explain how you intend to attract customers.

8) Screen 8: Milestones. List here key events in your plan over three years. For example: Year 1. Acquire 1,000 customers and £10,000 turnover.

9) Screen 9: Competition. List your competition here. Explain why what you offer is better and different.

10) Screen 10: Business model. Explain here how you intend to make money.

11) Screen 11: Financial. Explain how you have financed to date. If you have self-financed or 'Bootstrapped', say so here.

12) Screen 12: State how much cash you are looking for and your exit strategy.

13) Screen 13: Detail and explain here your exit strategy. How will your investor get their money back!

The slides should be a guide to what you are talking about (your pitch). Do not just read what is on the slides. You should be passionate about what you are presenting and show you have the determination and fire in your belly. Have fun with your presentation.

If you have a physical product you can show a demo. If it is web-based, be prepared and have a hard-drive copy. Be prepared for the internet connection dying at the crucial point! Practise your pitch so you know it inside out.

For You

You need to ensure you not only present your business, but also yourself, effectively. Wear a good suit and look professional. You have 30–90 seconds to create a good impression. Non-verbal communication is key.

Watch your hand gestures and how you stand. Make sure you are giving positive signals. Try to maintain eye contact with the audience. Make sure you are well groomed – is a haircut necessary? If you are going to be presenting under strong lighting, is make-up required? Make sure you are comfortable –avoid anything too tight, wear smart and loose-fitting clothing, polish your shoes!

Once you have presented your idea, you need to be ready for the questions. Here is a list of potential questions investors may ask:

1) What's your business all about? Give them something quick and catchy.

2) What is the barrier of entry to the competition?   Here, you're looking at: trademarks, patents, large start-up capital, a unique idea that is not easily replicated, your existing market share, if any.

3) Why are you raising the money you want? Explain to them how you arrived at your numbers and clarify what you will spend the money on.

4) How far will that money go? How long will the cash last if you have zero revenue (burn rate).

5) Do you have existing customers? If not, clarify how you will get them and give evidence that they exist.

6) What's your marketing strategy?

7) How are you going to scale the business?

8) More information about your team or background.

9) What happens if the company does not achieve the targets you've presented?

Offer an exit strategy or plan B if all does not go to plan.

Obviously, the number of potential questions is endless, so be prepared. Don't go for a chat; you only get *one* chance with an investor. Don't be late, don't be evasive, answer all questions directly and tell the truth. If you don't know the answer to a question, say so, but say you will get back to him/her. Remember to ask about the investor too, it's not all one way! If the investor seems interested, remember to ask what will happen next. If things have gone well, they will ask for more information or another meeting.

MY STORY

MY STORY

Who Wants To Meet A Millionaire?

So, I prepared my business plan, my deck presentation slides and my summary business plan. I registered with a few angel investor websites and waited... After two months and no one biting, I checked my email one day and there it was – an email from an interested investor! Preliminary research showed him to be a multi-million pound businessman! He was interested in my summary proposal and wanted more in-depth information:

- Business plan
- CV
- Three years' accounts
- Professional advisors

All were required – very exciting! I promptly collated all the requested information in a one-file PDF document with my latest press coverage on the first page and hit 'send' on the email. Was this going to be the investor of my dreams? I did not know, but I had done all I could and would have to wait for either the dreaded rejection email or for the tantalising prospect of an investment meeting.

Days passed and I had heard nothing from the investor (not looking good). So I sent a polite reminder:
'Hello, just wondering if you received my plan, I've attached it again, just in case, many thanks.'

Three days passed and still nothing, then on the fourth day, there it was, the email from the investor stood out highlighted in bold in my inbox. I stared at the email subject line, a myriad of hopes and dreams flooding my mind. Was it a rejection? Was it positive? I was hovering over the message with the mouse, ready to click it. I closed my eyes and clicked, praying for a positive response. My heart sank as I opened my eyes partially and read the first few lines:

'Dear Graham,
Thanks for your plan. I have some concerns about the figures therefore...'

I opened my eyes fully and they darted uncontrollably through the text and to the end of the email:

'I would, therefore, like to meet you to discuss the opportunity further. I will be in London the 25th of May if that is OK with you?'

Yessss! I let out a big shout of success and punched the air with my clenched fist. My first investment meeting!

Once I had calmed down, it suddenly dawned on me that I had exactly two weeks to prepare for the meeting; probably the most important meeting of my life! The two weeks were spent preparing my documents. I bought a heat binder and bound my full-colour business plan to make everything as professional as possible. I also made sure there were logos on everything I printed. The pack included:

> 1) A hard copy of the original plan I had submitted.
>
> 2) A hard copy of my presentation deck in full colour.
>
> 3) A hard copy of the original summary business plan.

I transferred the presentation to my portable notebook computer and practised, practised, and practised some more.
The location was to be a very posh hotel around the corner from Buckingham Palace! I dry-cleaned my best suit and invested in a new pair of shoes for the occasion. The night prior to the meeting, I literally slept for two hours and was wide awake at 3am in the morning, so I used the opportunity to go over my figures and cement them in my mind:

> Turnover Year 1
> Turnover Year 2
> Turnover Year 3
> Gross profit Years 1, 2, 3

Net profit Years 1, 2, 3

I also committed to memory all my main costs:

Marketing costs – check
Own drawings – check
Staff costs – check

I practised my pitch, complete with slides on my computer once more. Was I ready? I hope I was!

After four hours of no sleep, I got ready to leave, put on the suit and checked off the items required in my A4 notepad:

1) Printed presentation deck – OK
2) Printed business plan – OK
3) Printed summary – OK
4) Business card – OK
5) Pen – OK
6) Notebook computer – OK
7) Charger for computer – OK
8) Brain! – OK

It would take around 45 minutes to get there, but I left one and a half hours early just to be sure. I felt very excited and surprisingly, only slightly nervous. I jumped on the London tube and the possibilities flooded my mind. Would I get an intense grilling? Would I go totally blank? Would I talk like a babbling idiot? Would I have to present to an audience? I hadn't asked, but I was prepared for anything.

Soon I had arrived at my destination, Victoria Station, and made the short walk to the venue. I walked past the location and took a good look as I passed as I was half an hour early. The hotel looked very posh, there was a black limousine parked outside and porters dressed in long black coat tails and black top hats – very, very posh. My nerve level shot up immediately. I decided to settle myself in a small café around the corner and ordered a glass of water and two bananas (brain food and instant energy), and took one last look at my plan and presentation. The time passed quickly and I made the short walk to the hotel, through the entrance past the porter and straight through to reception.'

'Hello,' I said politely, 'My name is Jules. I have a meeting with Mr Collard.' The receptionist picked up his phone and dialled, after a short while he spoke:

'A Mr Jules is here for you, Sir. OK, bye, bye.'

He placed the handset down and spoke to me. 'He will be with you in a while, please make your way to the lounge.' He gestured to a double door that was open. I could see an assortment of comfortable chairs and tables scattered in a large, but welcoming room. I walked through and sat down, scanning the room. 'Very plush, very expensive,' I thought to myself. The room was dotted with well-dressed ladies and men; some appeared deep in discussion, others relaxed as if on holiday. I picked up a newspaper and began to read. To be honest, I couldn't read the newspaper, my mind was too unsettled, but somehow, just holding the paper relaxed me.

Then I heard a voice: 'Hello, Mr Jules?' I looked up from my paper, 'Yes', I replied, 'Pleased to meet you!' My investor had arrived!

We walked over to a free table and sat down. 'A bit like a blind date, this,' I quipped. The investor smiled, his grey hair glinting in the light of the surprisingly hot May day.

'Do you want me to present? I've organised a presentation,' I put forward eagerly.

'Yes, OK,' said the investor. I promptly set up my notebook computer and went to the first slide and then the first line of my pitch:

'My name is Graham Jules, we provide creative spaces for creative people...'

The investor stopped me in mid-track. 'But please explain, what do you actually do? I have an idea but please explain in more detail,' he asked.

I proceeded to answer his question, he seemed satisfied with that and I tried to get back to my pitch... but was interrupted again.

'But tell me more about you, you've done a lot haven't you? It says so in your CV.'

'Yes,' I explained and gave a brief outline of my career to date.

The questions then came thick and fast:

'So why has this not been done before, then?' asked the investor, 'Who is your competition?' he added.

That was it, I decided to forget the pitch and just use the presentation slides to reinforce my answers.

'So how will you set up the premises?' asked the investor.

I skipped the presentation and showed him a location I had set up previously. 'And what about marketing? So you intend to grow the business via a franchise model? How do you intend to do that?'

The questions seemed relentless, but I answered all of them and eventually he seemed satisfied and asked me if I had any questions of my own. 'What businesses have you been involved with previously?' I asked. He replied that he had been involved in setting up large retail premises in the UK and Europe and also the fashion industry. 'Mmm, not a bad fit,' I thought.

And then that was it. We exchanged cards and the investor explained he would look through my pack and give me a decision within seven days. He explained that he sees around 100 people a year and usually invests in one, so my chances are only one in a 100! Using positive thinking to the max, not a huge number, I thought. He explained there would be a number of outcomes:

1) A second meeting to discuss.
2) A 'yes'.
3) A 'no'.

We shook hands, thanked each other for the meeting, and he walked away clutching my pack. I sat back in my chair and gave a big sigh of relief. It had gone well, and I was very, very excited. I could not believe I had just completed a meeting with a multi-million pound investor, but I had!

Lessons To Be Learned

So, what did I learn from the experience?

1) Be flexible with your pitch and be prepared for interruptions or to be taken off-track. Do not ignore the questions and carry on as rehearsed. Answer the investor's questions there and then.

2) Be polite – be humorous if you can!

3) Know your stuff. Do not assume the investor will have an exact idea of what your business is about, despite receiving your full plan.

4) If the investor is asking lots of questions, don't panic; that's a good thing, they just need more clarification.

5) At the end of the meeting, hand over your plan, the summary, and a printed version of your presentation, and get some idea of when you will find out the outcome.

6) Don't be too obsessed with the figures. (Know them, but don't assume that's the be-all and end-all.)

7) Be prepared that the investor will use the meeting to assess you personally, your character, and how you cope under pressure. They will decide whether they can work with you or not, so don't be defensive or argumentative.

The Answer

Two days passed, and one morning I looked at my email and saw the familiar subject and title from my prospective investor:

'Oh, no!' I thought, 'Why is he emailing already? Is it a no?'

I opened the email and read it tentatively: 'It was a pleasure meeting you, and thanks for the meeting, I will be looking over your documents and will have an answer for you between 7–14 days.'

'Phew!' I thought, 'still in the running!' A good sign – I think I passed the personality test at least!

I replied to the email: 'It was a pleasure meeting you too and I look forward to your reply…' I hit 'send' and crossed my fingers, praying for a positive result.

Weeks passed and I had not heard a thing from the investor. I decided to do a follow-up call. I nervously dialled the international number the investor had given me. The dial tone seemed to go on for an age… 'Hello,' a voice on the end of the line bellowed.

'Hello', I responded. 'It's Graham Jules, we met in London regarding my business proposal.'

'Ahhh, yes, Graham', responded the investor, 'Graham, I still have not decided yet, I will send you an email within the next few days.'

'Thanks very much', I said, relieved, and put the phone down. 'Wow, at least he's thinking about it,' I thought.

Two days later I checked my email and there it was – an email from the investor, I clicked on the message to open it:

'Graham, I have been researching your project and I believe it will be a difficult market to grow in. I am going to decline your offer to be involved, but wish you every success for the future, Kind regards…'

'Aghhhh, failure,' I thought, temporarily deflated.

I guess it would be nice to get investment from my very first investment meeting – that would be like a dream and a great ending to a book! But it wasn't to be; the disappointment was tinged with relief. At least I knew where I stood and had the vital experience of meeting and pitching to a real-life millionnaire investor. I guess the key to getting what you want is to persevere and learn from past experience, and to turn failures into positive outcomes. With that in mind, I proceeded to send my proposals to another 20 investors.

Big Plans

The next day, I opened my email and great! Another response from an investor:

'Graham, thanks for sending me your materials. I can't see why you would want £68,000. I would be surprised if this was ready to be franchised soon, wouldn't it need some national/regional customers? I find the whole proposition a bit unconvincing as it stands.'

'God, this guy is ripping everything apart, another rejection' I thought. I was about to close the email when I glanced at the last few lines:

'But, I can see business sense in principle. I love that you have bootstrapped the thing over the last few years. If I haven't completely p*ssed you off with my criticisms, I would be happy to share a cup of coffee with you to see whether there is a germ of an idea to invest in, Best regards…'

Yes! A day after being rejected, I had found another investor willing to meet and discuss the project, great! I patted myself on the back. It had paid off to continue regardless of the disappointment of the previous investor. This new investor was definitely direct! I could see this one was going to be a challenge, but I was on track, that was the main thing.

The second investor's approach was rather different. No swanky hotel foyers here.

We met outside my Hackney premises and headed to a local greasy spoon! Definitely down to earth, we discussed the project there. It was July when I first met this investor and fast forward three months, the beginning of October 2012, we were still in discussions, with three meetings, loads of emails and spreadsheets going back and forth. This guy was very thorough and wanted to reconcile all my past figures, accounts, different scenarios for different sales income of the business.

He had also found a couple of potential clients and was working on a new revised proposal with robust figures to attract other investors; very promising indeed, but still no offer as yet. I emailed my final set of figures and proposals and awaited his decision. My gut told me that surely no one would do this amount of work (three months worth) and then walk away? Only time would tell, I guess…

After what was literally months of to-ing and fro-ing over spreadsheets, figures, and projections, the investor's assessment of my proposal was complete:

He would like to invest! But with another investor, aghhh!?

Kind of a celebratory moment, but not! Another investor could be as difficult to find as the first one. The search continued…

Caught in limbo, I then proceeded to scour the internet for any kind of business funding I could set my eyes on:

- Angel networks
- Business loan funds
- Micro-financing for small business
- Small business foundations
- Venture capital

I searched and sent my summary proposal to as many as I could find. One day while searching, I came across a foundation whose aim was to help small businesses that were struggling to raise finance. I definitely ticked that box! I called the number on the website and enquired if I had a hope in hell of getting any funding! I was told to fill in the online form and an application pack would be sent to me and to return it. I would then be contacted within 14 days.

The application pack arrived in my inbox shortly afterward and I eyed at the documents required:

- Application form
- Business plan
- Cash flow forecast
- Corporate tax return
- Credit report
- Personal survival budget
- Rejection letter from own bank
- Six months' business bank statements
- Six months personal statements
- Three years' accounts

Wow! A massive list. Undeterred, I ticked off each requirement one by one in my A4 notebook. Fortunately, my dealings with the previous investor had forced me to have a detailed idea of cash flow and business plans. I had already been rejected by my own bank, so I had that in place. My accounts were up to date, so was the tax return. My credit file was almost clear and had minimal debt, so my file was OK. Six months' personal and business statements was fine, I downloaded these from my online banking. The personal survival budget was straight-forward as I had hardly anything to survive on!

I collected all the information and posted it recorded delivery. Three days later, my phone rang as I was working at my desk. It was a number I didn't recognise and I was currently being blitzed by sales calls:

'Who's that?' I asked brusquely

'Hello, is that Graham?' the voice said excitedly.

'Who's that?' I said again, losing patience.

'Oh, it's Margie, from the foundation'

'Ahh, yes,' my tone softened, as I realised it was not a sales call.

'I received your application and I like your plan, can you come in on Wednesday to discuss it further?'

'Yes!' I replied excitedly, 'Yes I can…'

Foundations

Wednesday arrived and I was on my way to the office of the foundation. I rang the entry bell at the large blue gates.

'Hello, my name's Graham Jules, I have a meeting with Margie.'

'Oh yes, come in, she's not here yet, but will be with you shortly,' said a female voice. The door clicked open and a small lady wearing dark-rimmed glasses appeared and showed me to the meeting room. Ten minutes passed, I checked my mobile to look at the time. 'Ahhh, better put my phone on silent,' I thought to myself and started prodding at the buttons. Before I could complete the operation, the doors were flung open:

'Hello, I'm Margie, sorry I'm late.'

Margie was the coordinator for the foundation, she would decide if I was to proceed further. The meeting was thorough but friendly. Questions about the usual suspects ensued: cash flow projections, assumptions, marketing, etc. My experience with previous investors allowed me to answer these questions with confidence.

After about 40 minutes the meeting was over. Margie spoke, 'I am not saying yes for definite, but I like what I see and it's positive. I will look at these figures some more and arrange a meeting with our funding panel. If you get through the funding panel, we will tell you if you are successful within ten minutes of completion of the panel meeting. So please keep next week Wednesday free as the panel will be meeting then.'
'That's great!' I beamed, 'Thanks for meeting me.' I shook Margie's hand and exited the building elated. Yesss! Funding panel, here I come!

THE FUNDING PANEL

21 Questions

I arrived at the plush offices of the City law firm, adjusted my tie, and went through the revolving doors. The place was huge, the receptionist sat there eager to help, I approached:

'Hello I'm Graham Jules. I'm here for the funding panel with Law & Co.'

'OK,' she replied, 'here's your card, sign there and it's on the thirteenth floor.'

'Thank you,' I replied and made my way to the hi-tech barriers. I placed my card on the top surface of the barrier and was automatically let through to the lift area.

'Very, hi-tech,' I thought, 'very, very smart.'

Onwards to the lift area, I was faced with an array of glass lifts and space-age type touch-screens from which you pre-ordered your desired lift. 'God, how do I work these?' I thought, and just then a lift arrived, the doors opened, and I made a short run and jumped in. Inside stood a man in late fifties, slightly grey, slim and quite tall.

'I need to get to the thirteenth floor,' I gasped, glancing around the lift, for the lift buttons and noticed there were no lift buttons!

'Sorry, erm, there are no buttons, how do I get there?' I asked, confused.

'It's OK,' he replied, 'I'm going there as well, these lifts got me too the first time, very hi-tech!' 'Yes,' I replied, and we laughed.

Once at the thirteenth floor, we both approached the receptionists. There were three of them and they sat behind huge Apple Mac screens.

'I'm here for the panel meeting with the foundation,' we both said at the same time! I glanced over and at that moment realised that the man in the lift was one of the panel members.

We were both twenty-five minutes early, and were shown by the receptionist to our meeting room, meeting room four. The room was large and plush, with stunning views of the London skyline. There was a fancy coffee machine with all kinds of up-market options and a plethora of snacks and nibbles.

The man spoke: 'You must be Graham? I'm Garry, the owner and main financier of the foundation, pleased to meet you.'

I was gob-smacked. Here I was faced with the main decision maker, the guy with the cash and had at least 10–15 minutes before anyone else would arrive. 'Quick, Graham, make a good impression and fast!' I thought to myself.

We chatted politely and he explained that as an investor in businesses he liked to meet potential business owners face-to-face, rather than decide on the basis of paperwork alone.

'Great idea, great idea', I gushed.

After about ten minutes, another panel member arrived and I was ushered out into the reception area again. Ten minutes after that, everyone had arrived. There were six panel members including Garry and my coordinator Margie. My time had come!

I sat in reception and seemed to be waiting for an age. I didn't feel *that* nervous, but I hate waiting. Eventually, Margie shot out of the meeting room, 'Right, Graham, the panel is ready for you.'

'OK', I replied, stood up and walked confidently into the room.

'Hello, everyone,' I announced, trying to get eye contact with all six panel members.

'Hello,' they all replied in unison.

The meeting started easily enough. 'So, tell me about the business so far, Graham,' asked one of the panel members. I was very comfortable talking about what I had achieved so far and was opening up and telling a good story. Then the barrage arrived:

'So, Graham, tell us about your accounts, you've made minimal profit so far; can you tell us why?'

'Why do you expect profitability to change?'

'Do you have your accounts with you?'

'No', I replied 'Sh*t!' I thought to myself, 'I've left the bloody accounts at home!'

'So, Graham, how do you intend to market the venture?'

The questions were intrusive, intense, and very penetrating. I tried to remain calm and reply the best I could. My body heat must have shot up 20 degrees during the 45-minute dissection of me and my business. Then suddenly, it was over. I gave an internal sigh of relief; I had made it, survived the panel intact –well, almost.

'So, Graham, if you want to leave the room and wait in reception, the panel will come to a decision,' said Garry the head panel member. I walked out with Margie and fell into the plush sofa, energy drained and exhausted.

'How do you think I did?' I asked Margie nervously.

'You did well, nothing bad at all,' she answered.

'Apart from forgetting to bring the accounts!' I retorted. We both laughed nervously.

After 15 minutes in reception, one of the panel members walked out and called us back in. Garry was sitting in his chair, leaning back slightly.

'OK, Graham,' he began, 'we feel your accounts are obtrusive, we feel it's a risky venture, and I'm not prepared to take all the risk…'

My heart sank, another rejection. 'Oh well, at least I tried,' I thought. Garry continued:

'If you can get us your latest accounts – when are your next accounts due?'

'Erm, oh they're not due until July, in five months,' I answered.

'Oh', replied Garry a little angrily, 'if I had an offer I would get the accounts over ASAP,' he snapped.

'I have an offer?' I asked, surprised.

'Yes, you have an offer, we are not prepared to take all the risk, but we will fund 50% of the project, so you will have to get the rest from somewhere, just get us those accounts. Well done, Graham!' His tone had changed.

Wow, I could not believe it, I'd done it! I was convinced it was a rejection, but in a stunning turnaround I'd come out with 50% funding.

'Thank you so much, thank you,' I said excitedly as I shook all the panel members' hands. I left the building smiling broadly; yes, at last, things were changing for the better.

Panel Tips

1) Arrive early. Arriving early meant I had a unique opportunity to sell myself to the head panel member! Don't be late.

2) Be prepared. Bring your accounts, photos, figures, cash flow, etc. Do not assume they will have it, even if you've sent it. I forgot the accounts - big mistake - and was lucky.

3) Clean up your act. Make sure any nasties are taken care of and explainable: CCJs, your credit file, any court disputes, etc. Any investor is 99% likely to pull this from the public record. They do not expect you to be perfect, but whatever you do, do not lie or try to hide anything onerous or they will write you off straight away.

4) Be friendly but professional. Ensure you greet everyone personally on the panel. Shake all hands and make eye contact. Try to get all the panel members on your side by greeting and acknowledging them all, even if they look super scary!

THE £250,000 PRESENTATION

Never Gonna Give You Up

I'd contacted over 1,000 individual investors, angel groups, and venture capital firms, and had success with an offer of some funding under my belt. It was December, Christmas was on its way (two weeks away, to be exact), and my plan was to stop actively fundraising, as I had spent the last nine months trying and I wanted to concentrate on expanding the business in the New Year.

The fundraising process was very time-consuming. Emails, meetings with investors, telephone discussions, preparation of plans, and numerous rejections. So, to be honest, it was a bit of a pleasure to be winding down and I was looking forward to relaxing over Christmas with a few mince pies in hand!

Then, one day, I received a phone call: 'Hello,' the voice said, 'is that Graham?'

'Yes,' I said, 'who's that?'

'Oh, my name's Bill. I received your business plan, it looks very interesting'.

'OK,' I said, tentatively. I'd sent so many proposals I had no idea who this guy was. 'What's your company, who are you with?' I asked.

'Well, I represent a group of angel investors, they meet once in a while and there is an opportunity to present to a room full of angel investors; would you like to be put forward?'

I was a bit stunned, so much for a quiet Christmas! 'Yes,' I said enthusiastically, 'that would be fantastic'.

'Great,' said Bill excitedly, 'I'll send you an email. The first step is to meet you to discuss your plan. How's the New Year, say January, looking for you? Can't do anything sooner due to Christmas slowing everything down!' We both laughed. 'Yes, yes, that's fine', I replied. 'Perfect'.

'Wow,' I thought, 'what a result.' I sat down at my laptop and searched for Bill – he was number 311 on the list! I'd submitted my plan for investment a couple of months ago; it was for my full expansion plan for £250,000 investment: FANTASTIC!

Very Important People

Xmas had been and gone, it was cold, it was snowy, and it was the second week of January 2013. I looked out of the window and fresh white snow coated the rooftops. 'What a cold miserable morning for an investment meeting!' I thought. 'Will the trains even be running?' To be honest, I was not in the mood for it at all. I searched the internet for trains to my destination in the suburbs and was disappointed to find all the trains running. Damn, I guess I'll have to turn up. I wasn't feeling positive at all!

I tentatively stepped out into the snow and made my way to the station. I was making good progress then, thwack! Next thing I knew, I was flat on my back on the pavement, my black file box still clutched in my hand as though my life depended on it. Ouch, what a morning. I stood up slowly. 'God that hurt,' I thought to myself.

'Are you OK?' asked a sympathetic passing couple.

'I'm OK, thanks', I replied weakly.

'Go slowly, it's slippery here,' added the lady of the pair.

'Yes,' I replied, 'Great start to the morning eh? Almost breaking my back.' I added ironically. They smiled.

'At least you're OK' she added

'Thank you,' I said and made my way, very slowly, to the station.

Once at my destination I entered the reception area. 'Have a seat,' said the receptionist, 'Bill will be with you in a minute.'

A minute later, Bill arrived. He shook my hand firmly, 'Hello Graham, how are you?' he said in a brisk northern tone.

'I'm fine,' I said, 'apart from almost breaking my back in the snow!' We laughed.

'Walk this way, Graham; I'll introduce you to my colleague Sandra.'

We went through to the meeting room I shook hands with his colleague, Sandra. They both seemed very friendly, Bill a friendly northerner, and Sandra a blonde, serious but approachable businesswoman, not scary at all. They had quite a lot of banter and joke-telling going on.

'Quite a relaxed setting,' I thought.

Then Sandra explained, 'So Graham, this is how it works. We hold an investment club for our angel investors once every few months. We select six businesses to present to – there is no charge to present. The first step is to put you forward. We will put forward nine businesses out of all the businesses that have approached us, and then those nine will be cut down to six. So, tell me about your business.'

I gulped, 'Erm. Shall I present?' I began to pull out the laptop.

'Oh, no.' said Sandra, 'just talk off the top of your head.'

'OK, then.' I replied.

Luckily, all the experience of pitching to the foundation and investors had meant I knew my pitch pretty well and I began talking confidently. I finished and they looked at each other.

'What do you think?' said Bill to Sandra, 'Shall we let him through?' 'Yes, yes,' said Sandra.

'Great!' I thought, trying not to look overly pleased with myself. Bill continued:
'You will have to put together a presentation of your plan; I will email you with the templates for a PowerPoint presentation. You will use this to present to us again next month, and if all is good, we will put you forward to the pre-selection **stage,** where

you will present to a couple of the head investors of the club.'

'Thanks so much for this,' I said, my excitement brimming over. I said my goodbyes and made my way out of the building. It was worth going to the cold, snowy, investment meeting after all.

Million Dollar Plan

A few days later the presentation templates had landed in the inbox, I clicked and opened the files. I had already created my presentation file, but needed to edit it to meet the investment club's criteria: The template read:

1) The entire plan presentation should not be more than ten minutes.

2) Each slide should contain no more than seven bullet points and contain a maximum seven words per bullet point.

3) Your product: Don't go into too much detail about your product, less is more.

4) Don't say the market is worth x million and we aim to take x% of it.

5) Financials: How will you earn money? How will you reach your market?

6) Team: Who is the team and what experience do they have?

7) Competition: Barriers to entry, why would people buy your product or service?

8) Investment: How much money do you need? What will you do with the money?

9) Exit strategy: Who will buy the company and why? How much will the investor make?

I went about editing my presentation deck to meet the criteria and wrote a presentation script for each slide and practised. Before I knew it, January had ended and February had arrived. It was the day of my first presentation to Bill and Sandra from the investment club. To be honest, I was nervous; the presentations looked large and bold on the projection screen. I toyed with the remote control to ensure it operated fluidly.

'OK,' said Bill, 'we will time you, so begin when you are ready.'

I began, my mouth was dry, but this was it, I went for it. The first few slides went well, then, presentation disaster, the slides went blank. I frantically played with the remote while continuing to spout the memorised pitch. After what seemed an age, the projector burst into life again and I continued to the end of my presentation.

'OK, good,' said Bill, 'that was OK, it was eight minutes long, under ten minutes, so that's good.' He paused, then continued. 'We're going to give you some feedback; we're going to be blunt, so please don't take offence'

'That's OK.' I said slightly worried, 'Better now than in front of the investors!' I joked flatly.

Sandra continued: 'Right, here are my points:

1) Do not talk to the screen or step in front of it.

2) Change your nervousness into passion – be positive.

3) Focus on the investable opportunity.

4) Your slides are too busy: bullet points rather than sentences.

5) Mention your future team.

6) Include a competitor grid.

7) On your exit strategy, give an example, if possible, of who the business will sell to. Our investors prefer a business that will sell for a multiple of EBITDA (earnings before interest, taxes, depreciation, and amortization). Give them a figure rather than 8–10 times return.

'All in all, not bad. If you make those changes, we will be happy to put you forward to the pre-selection panel with the investors in March.'

'Valuable advice,' I thought. 'That's fantastic, I'll make the changes.' I could not believe it – I was only two more steps away from presenting to a room full of 70 angel investors and asking for two hundred and fifty grand!

The Three Angels

So, there I was, standing in front of three angel investors and Sandra. It was the beginning of March, but still cold, no sign of spring. I was feeling surprisingly calm. I had arrived early, had something to drink, and had rehearsed my pitch on the train. I'd even managed to be light-humoured on my entrance to the meeting room and prepared myself to deliver my well-rehearsed presentation. Here was the chance I had been waiting for; after this, I would be presenting to a room full of 70 high net worth individuals, any one of whom could change my life forever! I poured a small glass of water and drank, I felt good and ready to deliver:

'OK, Graham, you can begin when you're ready.'

'Ok,' I said, making one last clearance of my throat and began: 'My name is Graham Jules, my company provides creative spaces for creative people. Erm...' I paused and stuttered, trying quickly to make my mouth connect to my brain, 'My name is Graham Jules... Erm. God, what was happening? I couldn't get the words out or remember anything other than my name!

'My name is Graham and... Errr.' My temperature started to rise and I could do nothing, I just stood there – damn. There was an awkward silence in the room for what seemed to be an age, then one of the investors pitched in:

'Graham, we are here to help you, please feel free to try again.' I calmed myself, took a deep breath and delivered my pitch flawlessly.

'We will be in touch.' said Sandra flatly as I left the meeting room shortly afterwards. I was despondent; what the hell had happened to me? I literally couldn't speak, a real awkward *'Dragons Den'* moment. I tried to remain positive. Surely they can see past the temporary brain lapse? Would I be penalised on my presentation skills? All I could do was wait with trepidation for the result via email.

Sure enough, a week later there it was in the inbox, the email I had been waiting for. I stabbed at it with the mouse quickly as if it was an irritating pest I wanted to get out of the way. The email opened, my eyes darted over the first line:

'Dear Graham, we are pleased to inform you that you have been selected to present to the investor club.'

My heart raced and adrenaline rushed through my veins, the feeling of elation was fantastic, I had not messed it up after all and I was going to present to a room full of angels. Reee-sult!

The Final Countdown

Three weeks later and my time had come; it was the day before my investment presentation. I tried to reflect on my previous presentation efforts, in particular my 'brain lapse incident,' and tried to find a solution. It occurred to me that I was probably too relaxed that day and over-rehearsed. I cast my mind back at the moment my mouth stopped working and realised I hadn't breathed from the moment I took the projector remote in my hand! My poor brain was probably starved of oxygen! I made a mental note to take some breaths prior to speaking this time. I also decided to 'pump myself up mentally' and not to allow myself to get too laid back and utilise any nerves I was feeling to propel the presentation forward. I made a further mental note to bring some energy food (bananas, nuts and a caffeine-free energy drink) that I could consume a few hours before my presentation to give me more added oomph.

On a practical note, I printed off all the usual documents. I printed off a few copies of the presentation for any interested investors and made two posters that could be displayed on my stand after I had presented. I came ready prepared with business plan and accounts that could be shown if requested, and brought some business cards and a one-page summary of the proposal that could also be displayed. I also checked the PowerPoint presentation was up to date with all changes intact. I practised a couple of times that night, avoiding over-rehearsing and went to bed.

In the morning I woke up refreshed, packed all of my materials, my laptop, practised two more times, and left fully ready for action. I arrived at my destination and headed for the presentation hall.

The location was different from the previous rehearsals: a large meeting room with about 12 rows of chairs.

Bill was there with Sandra. I entered quietly as another business was about to deliver their practise pitch and I sat down. The other business owner delivered his pitch; it was fairly well delivered, although a tad over the 10-minute requirement.

'Graham, your turn next,' announced Bill.

I sat upright in my seat, caught slightly by surprise that I had to deliver so quickly. I took a few short breaths and made my way up to the projector. I began and as I spoke, I felt good. The few people who were in the room looked on and I tried to make eye contact. All was well, until the projector decided to skip slides all by itself. 'Damn technology!' I thought to myself, and adjusted the slides with the remote and carried on, getting to the end flawlessly.

'Well done!' said Bill 'Next, please go downstairs to set up your stand and be back here in a couple of hours to do it for real!'

I headed downstairs to the large restaurant that had been hired specifically for the event and set up my stand. I placed my printed presentations on the tables provided and all my other presentation materials and hooked up my laptop with a short repeating presentation of some graphics and key points of my presentation. The stand looked good, the event looked promising, and the other five business owners looked very professional. What would the investors have to say? I didn't have to wait long to find out.

The two hours flew by, I had already gone back upstairs to the presentation room and I could see a couple of the investors had arrived and were milling about in another room. I grabbed my 'goody bag' of nuts, energy drink and bananas, and ate them, then made my way to the bathroom. As I entered, I noticed there was a man in there. He was short – about 5' 5" –and wearing prescription sunglasses.

'Hello', I said politely.

'Hello', he replied.

'Are you here to present at the event?' I asked.

'No,' he replied, 'I'm here as an investor, my name's Tom.'

'Ahh, hello Tom, my name's Graham Jules, nice to meet you.' Typical, I thought, great place to meet an investor, in the toilets minutes before the presentation!

'Oh, yes, I wanted to talk to you,' said Tom excitedly. 'I saw your summary and thought it was interesting and wanted to ask you a few questions.'

'Go ahead,' I answered, thinking on my feet. Tom proceeded to ask some questions about the business, which I answered and he seemed satisfied.

'Great!' he exclaimed, 'we'll talk after the presentation.'

'Talk about "always be prepared",' I thought. I'd just pitched informally to the first investor in the bathroom! Now bring on the presentation!

The meeting room was packed full of investors, the vast majority of the 12 rows of chairs were filled, the front rows being reserved for the businesses presenting. I made my way to my seat and sat down. After the formalities, the first presentation stood up ready to present. He made his way to the projector and Bill went to the laptop to start the first presentation slide, then, disaster. His PowerPoint file could not be found. Bill searched the desktop to see if he could find it but it was nowhere to be seen. I selfishly scanned the projector screen to check if I could see *my* presentation and sure enough, it was there on the desktop with one other (phew!), but all the others had vanished. Bill became very red, and frantically pushed at the laptop buttons for what seemed like an age. The investors were dead quiet in the room, not a sound. Then eventually, relief.

'Right!' said Bill, in his northern tone, 'Slight technical hitch, but we're ready to go now.'

The first business began and it was not long before it was my turn. I stood up, made my way to the projector, grabbed the projector remote, took a few short breaths of air into my lungs and began: 'Hello, my name is Graham Jules, I am here to present my company…' My voice seemed loud and booming in the room and I felt energised with confidence, I was feeling good and the investors seemed to be looking on intently. I finished and the applause rang out.

I had made it, presented to a room full of investors. The sense of relief rushed over me – a great feeling. I felt elated, and relieved at the lack of technical hitches, but also nervous in anticipation of the live feedback I was about to receive from the multi-millionaire investors.

After the last business had finished, we all headed downstairs to the restaurant and our business stands where we could chat to the investors from the club. There was wine, champagne, and canapés available; very nice. The investors trickled in, one by one. I stood at my stand, intently waiting for the feedback, dismissing offers of wine; I didn't want to get too sloshed prior to answering their questions!

'Very good presentation', one investor offered.

'Great idea', offered another.

'It has great potential,' said another.

I collected cards and email addresses from the investors I had spoken to and handed out the presentation summaries. The evening continued with many promising comments, but nothing concrete in terms of an offer of investment and after about an hour, the evening had come to an end. One of the coordinators named Joy came over to me.

'How did it go?' she asked.

'Yes, it went well, very positive feedback on the presentation', I replied, 'but nothing concrete yet. Let's see if anyone gets back.'

'Yes, I think you did well', replied Joy, 'we give them feedback forms once they leave the presentation room upstairs – let's see what those say.'

'OK', I replied, slightly disappointed. Although I was glad of the experience and positive feedback, deep down I really wanted that indication of investment interest, just one investor that would say out loud they would consider investing in my company. But it was not to be, I packed up my stand and materials, slightly relieved it was over and very glad for the experience. I thanked all those who had given me the chance – Bill, Sandra, and Joy – and left wondering what the future might hold. Deep down, I was not holding my breath for a result from the presentation, but at least I had done it and had successfully managed to present my ideas to a room full of high net-worth individuals.

Two weeks later I checked my email and saw an email from Joy. The subject read: 'Investment Club Feedback'. I clicked on the email and opened the attachment. I was faced with a list of about twenty names with comments beside each name.

The feedback forms had arrived. I eyed the document un-emotionally, without expectation. 'Would you be interested in investing?' was one of the questions posed to the investors. I glanced down the list of names, one by one. 1) No, 2) No, 3) No, 4) No, 5) No....' 'Oh well,' I thought, 'at least they all rated my presentation skills very well.' Then my attention was caught by the eleventh name on the list: 'Quality of presentation 4/5, financial attractiveness 3/5, would you be interested in investing in the proposal? YES.' I read it again, this time with my finger pressed against the screen to make sure I had read the rows correctly: 'Would you be interested in investing in the proposal?' I *had* read correctly. YES, I read correctly!

There was one investor who was actually interested in investing in my company. I could not believe it, I was ecstatic, some real interest following my presentation – this was unbelievable! I quickly emailed Joy. I had not even spoken to this investor at the event. Within minutes Joy had replied – she would send my details to the investor to create a dialogue.

Whatever happened now, I was on the right path, to the right destination. The whole process had shown me that I was ready to put my business ideas forward. The confidence and power to approach angel investors was now in my grasp. I did not know what the future would hold with this investor or the others, but whatever it was, I knew it would be exciting!

I had gone from Business Zero to Superhero ®!

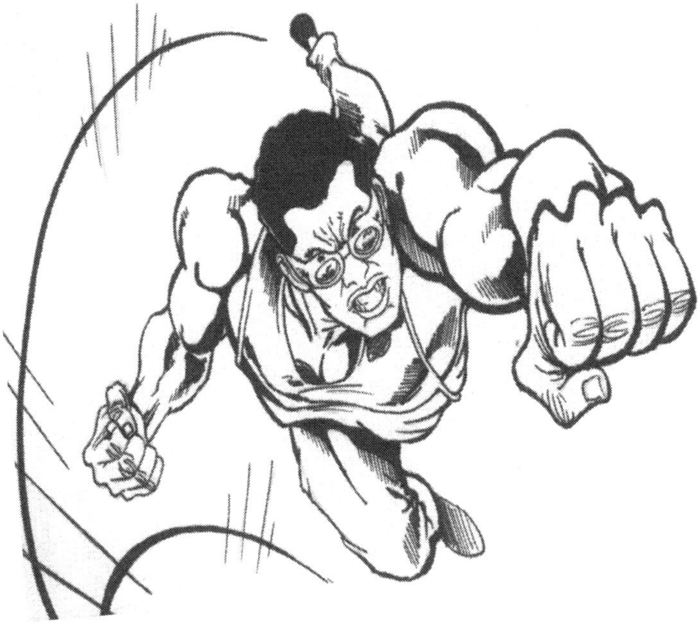

Comic Book Page 14

THE END

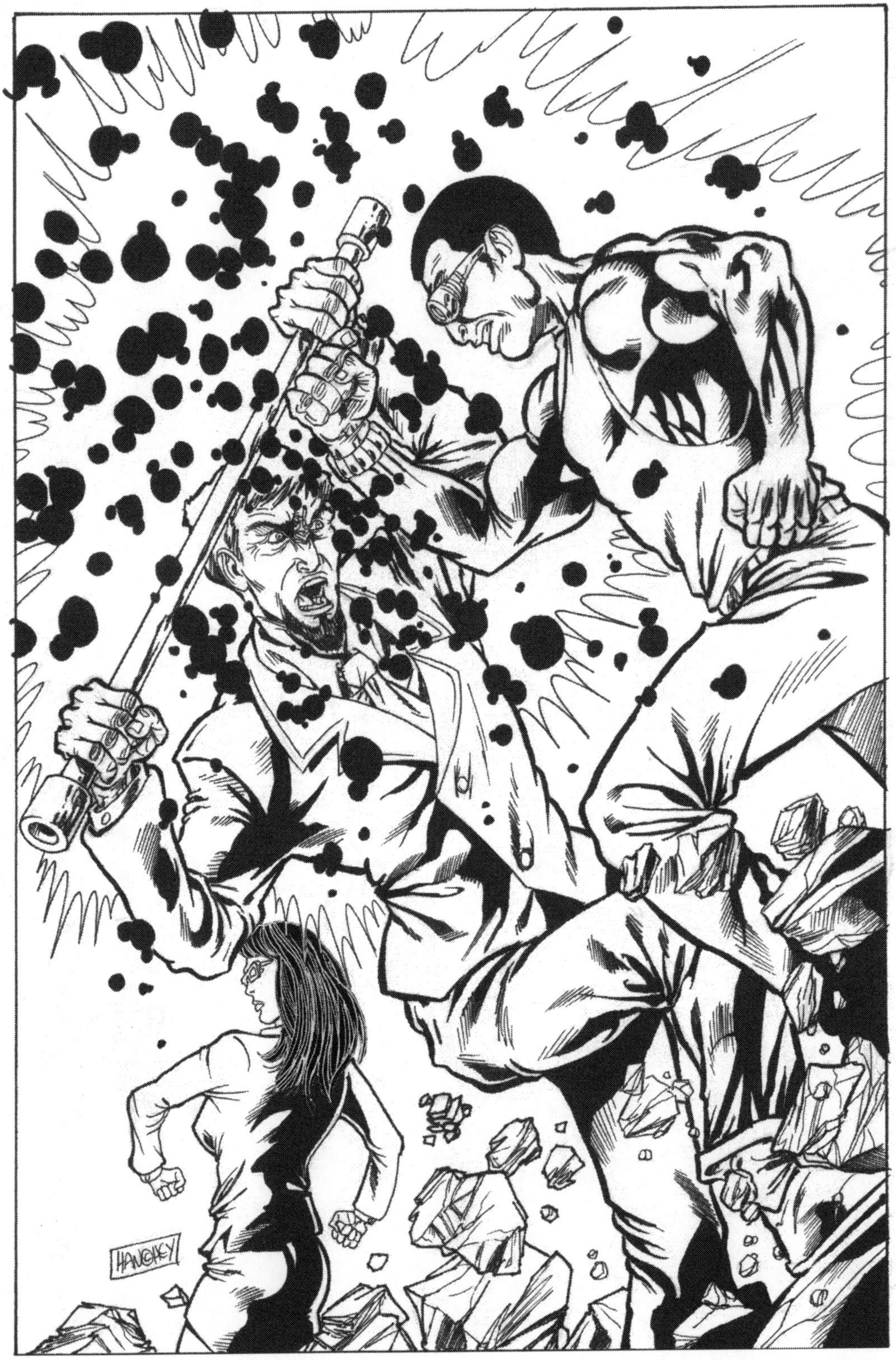
HANCHEY

ABOUT THE AUTHOR

The author, Graham Jules LL.B (Hons) is a Business Law graduate and British entrepreneur. His legal experience helped him win the trade mark for this very book against major entertainment company Marvel and DC Comics Entertainment Inc. The company opposed this book title BUSINESS ZERO TO SUPERHERO ®, due to their trade mark SUPERHEROES. Following a three-year battle, Graham's subsequent victory was reported in the national media and news, including the BBC and Sky.

He runs his own successful business, Pop Up World ®, a collection of pop-up spaces for creative people. In the 90's he produced various music acts and ran a record label Blam! Records. He has over twenty years experience in entrepreneurship and business development.

Graham's story proves that following his methods can aid success in business even against seemingly impossible odds. You too can transform from Business Zero To Superhero ® !

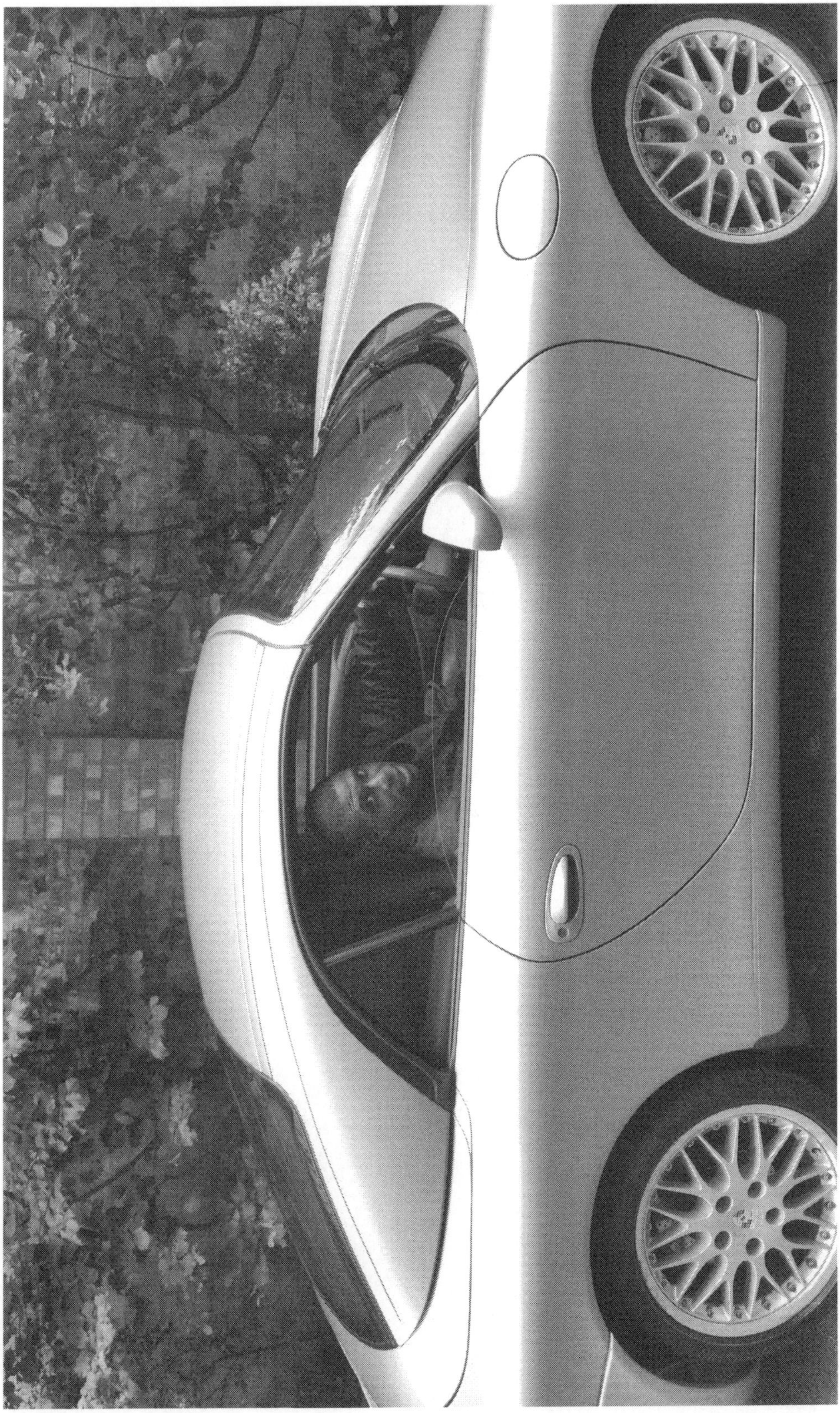

Contact Information:

info@businesszerotosuperhero.com

Notes:

Index

80–20 rule 115
AdSense 166
Advertising 86, 107
AdWords 89, 167, 168
agreements 174
Alexa 22
Angel Investors 181
Angel networks 206
annual accounts 169
annual returns 49
articles 140
Automation 161
Automation software 162
bank accounts 50
bank loans 170
Bank loans 58
bank statements 169
bankruptcy 69
barrier of entry 193
Barriers to entry 218
benefits office 58
blacklist 67
blogs 141
bootstrap 66
borrow money 67
burn rate 193
Business Banking Insight (BBI) 53
Business loan 206
business model 57, 67, 88
business plan 185, 186, 187, 190, 196, 197, 198, 214, 222
Business Rates 37

Business to Business Selling: 84
call to action 109
Cash flow forecast 206
CCJ 71
CDFIs 58
Certificate of Incorporation 50
Community development finance institutions 58
Companies Act 51, 52, 239
Companies House 49
Competition 192
Compound interest 177
contract law 98
conversion rate 96, 97, 98, 104, 107, 117, 161, 162, 165
Copyright 12, 144
Corporate tax return 206
correspondence 169
County Court Judgements 68, 70, 71
credit 68
credit agreements 70
credit file 67, 68, 69, 70, 71, 169, 207, 213
credit rating 69
credit reference agencies 70
credit score 61, 62, 66, 72, 73, 74, 76, 77, 78, 80
Credit unions 58
Crowd funding 59
CVs 186

Database 104
deck 185, 190, 191, 196, 197, 198, 218
Discounts 164
disputes 139, 174
Distance Selling Regulations 174
Distress 39
earnings before, interest, taxes, depreciation and amortization 220
eBay 58
EBITDA 220
electoral roll 68
Electoral Roll 76
email 109
Email Marketing 86
Employers Liability Insurance 173
Endorsements 140
Equifax 67
equity 188
exit strategy 220
Experian 67
Facebook 109
finance company 68
Floatation 183
franchise 163
free list of hundreds of investor contacts 184
Google 140, 141, 142, 150, 151, 153, 154, 166, 167
government 58
Grants 58
Headline 156
hire purchase 39, 40
HMRC 82

HTML 151
Intellectual Property 143
Intellectual Property Office 20, 146
Investments 59
IVA 76
journalist 157
keyword 141, 151, 152, 153, 154, 167
leads 96
license 163
limited company 28, 49, 50, 70, 103, 170, 185
limited liability 50
Linear income 47
link farms 153
LinkedIn 184
marketing strategies 87
Marketing Strategies 88
marketing strategy 86, 96, 161, 194
Marvel and DC 20, 21, 128, 131, 143, 145, 231
moderated web forum 141
multiple universes 126
N244 form 71
National Insurance 49, 54, 55
Non-Disclosure Agreements 146
online reputation management 142
Outsourcing 162
page ranking 153
Pareto 115
passive income 47
Passive residual income 47

Patent	143, 145	share dealing	176
PAYE	54	shareholders	59
peer to peer lenders	63	Small Business Rate Relief	38, 239
Performing Rights Society	144	Small Claims Court	100
Places for Business	166	social media	109
Power Point	190	sole trader	50
PR	142	solving problems	123
PR campaign	158	spam	110, 111, 185
press coverage	157	spread betting	176
Press Release	155, 157	**Stock Market**	182
Print media	155	stocks and shares	59
Private investors	59	Testimonials	139
proof of ID	174	The Town and Country Planning Act	92
Public Liability Insurance	173	to do' list	117
public relations	157	trade body	139
quantum physics	126	**Trade Mark**	143, 145, 239
Radio	155	TV	155
Rateable value	37	Twitter feeds	109
Real World Gallery	231	Up-sell	164
referrals	164	Valuation Office	30
registered office	51, 70	Valuing your business	188
Registered office	70	VAT	82
Repossession	38	VAT registered	169
reputation	139	VAT return	169
Schrödinger's Cat	126	**Venture Capital**	182
search engine	150	viral	108, 139
Search engine optimisation	141	Web spider	154
SEO	5, 141, 150, 151, 153, 154, 157, 167	webmaster	142
		ZX81	26

Bibliography

Articles / Journals:

2015 data from the Office for National Statistics licensed under the Open Government License v.3.0.

Bizarre imagery as an effective memory aid: The importance of distinctiveness. McDaniel, Mark A.; Einstein, Gilles O. Journal of Experimental Psychology: Learning, Memory, and Cognition, Vol 12(1), Jan 1986, 54-65

https://www.ncbi.nlm.nih.gov/pmc/articles/PMC3106157/

Prof Wayne Hall, Adverse health effects of non-medical cannabis use, The Lancet, http://www.thelancet.com/journals/lancet/article/PIIS0140-6736(09)61037-0/fulltext

Rothwell Carol and Cohen Pete (Happiness Report-January 2003), 'Happiness is no Laughing Matter'

Schifferstein HN, Talke KS, Oudshoorn DJ, Can Ambient Scent Enhance the Nightlife Experience?

UK & Ireland profit of $971m 2016 p130 Group Financial Statements https://www.experianplc.com/media/2733/experian-ar2016.pdf

Vilfredo Pareto, Cours d'économie politique (1896–97)

Cases:

Apple, Inc. v. Amazon.com Inc., Case No. CV 11-01327 PJH (N.D. Cal. July 6, 2011

Carlill v Carbolic Smoke Ball Company [1892] EWCA Civ 1

Fisher v Bell [1961] 1 QB 394

Gilford Motor Co Ltd v Horne [1933] Ch 935

Haughton Elevator Co. v. Seeberger, 85 U.S.P.Q. 80 (1950)

Salomon v Salomon & Co Ltd [1896] UKHL

Legislation:

Chapter 2 s22 Consumer Rights Act 2015
Chapter 3 -Consumer Rights Act 2015
Committee of Advertising Practice Code 3.2
Consumer Contracts (Information, Cancellation and Additional Charges) Regulations 2013
Data Protection Act 1998
Employers' Liability (Compulsory Insurance) Act 1969
s103 Law of Property Act 1925
s12 Sale of Goods Act 1979
s13 Supply of Good and Services Act 1982
s140A Consumer Credit Act – Unfair relationship test
s15a Sale of Goods Act 1979
s170-s177 Companies Act 2006
s220 Town and Country Planning Act 1990
s30 Landlord and Tenant Act 1925
s36 Administration of Justice Acts 1970
s53 Companies Act 2006
Section 388 Companies Act 2006
s86D Consumer Credit Act 1974
s90B Consumer Credit Act 1974
Sale of Goods Act 1979
Section 451 Companies Act 2006
The Companies (Late Filing Penalties) and Limited Liability Partnerships (Filing Periods and Late Filing Penalties) Regulations 2008

The Non-Domestic Rating (Small Business Rate Relief) (England) Order 2012
The Taking Control of Goods Regulations 2013
Trade Mark Act 1994

Websites:

http://hermes.ffn.ub.es/luisnavarro/nuevo_maletin/Schrodinger_1935_cat.pdf

http://loot.com/

http://www.alexanderaranda.com/about

http://www.drisk.it

http://www.experian.co.uk/

http://www.financial-ombudsman.org.uk/

http://www.financial-ombudsman.org.uk/publications/ombudsman-news/40/40_setoff.htm

http://www.genielending.co.uk/

http://www.primesight.co.uk/

http://www.prsformusic.com/Pages/default.aspx

http://www.simplybusiness.co.uk/about-us/press-releases/750,000-small-business-owners-missing-out-on-summer-holidays-with-children/

http://www.unc.edu/peplab/publications/Fredrickson%20AESP%202013%20Chapter.pdf

https://ads.twitter.com/login

https://angel.co/

http://british-business-bank.co.uk/

https://business.instagram.com/advertising?locale=en_GB

https://docsend.com

https://fleximize.com/

https://ico.org.uk/action-weve-taken/nuisance-calls-and-messages/

https://www.amazon.co.uk/Bacon-Smell-Fragrance-Sensory-Decisions/dp/B0118FAS1G

https://www.barclaycard.co.uk/business/making-payments/business-credit-cards

https://www.boostcapital.co.uk

https://www.cap.org.uk/Advertising-Codes/Broadcast.aspx

https://www.cap.org.uk/Advertising-Codes/Non-Broadcast.aspx

https://www.capitalontap.com

https://www.cifas.org.uk/nfd

https://www.creditcompass.co.uk/

https://www.creditexpert.co.uk/

https://www.crowdcube.com/

https://www.dwavesys.com/our-company/meet-d-wave

https://www.facebook.com/business/

https://www.facebook.com/business/products/ads

https://www.fairfinance.org.uk/business-loans/

https://www.fiverr.com/

https://www.fundingcircle.com/uk/

https://www.fundingxchange.co.uk/

https://www.google.co.uk/adwords/get-started/

https://www.gov.uk/apply-register-design

https://www.gov.uk/copyright

https://www.gov.uk/data-protection-register-notify-ico-personal-data

https://www.gov.uk/government/publications/rates-and-allowances-corporation-tax/rates-and-allowances-corporation-tax

https://www.gov.uk/how-to-register-a-trade-mark/apply

https://www.gov.uk/how-to-register-a-trade-mark/what-you-can-and-cant-register

https://www.gov.uk/income-tax-rates/current-rates-and-allowances

https://www.gov.uk/make-court-claim-for-money/court-fees

https://www.gov.uk/patent-your-invention

https://www.gov.uk/register-a-design

https://www.gov.uk/register-to-vote

https://www.gov.uk/self-employed-national-insurance-rates

https://www.gov.uk/tax-on-dividends/how-dividends-are-taxed

https://www.gov.uk/vat-rates

https://www.gov.uk/vat-registration-thresholds

https://www.gumtree.com/

https://www.ipo.gov.uk/p-apply-before.htm

https://www.ipo.gov.uk/p-ipsum.htm

https://www.iwoca.co.uk/

https://www.meetup.com/

https://www.moneyclaim.gov.uk/web/mcol/welcome

https://www.mybusinessprofile.com/

https://www.nominet.uk/domains/resolving-uk-domain-disputes-and-complaints/

https://www.ratesetter.com/

https://www.signkick.co.uk/

https://www.snapchat.com/l/en-gb/ads

https://www.startuploans.co.uk/

https://www.tax.service.gov.uk/view-my-valuation/search

https://www.ukclassifieds.co.uk/
https://www.xero.com/content/dam/xero/pdf/Xero-Make-or-break-report.pdf

https://www.youtube.com/watch?v=PqN_2jDVbOU

https://www.youtube.com/yt/advertise/en-GB/

https://www.youtube.com/yt/advertise/en-GB/

Printed in Great Britain
by Amazon